I0224342

The Witings of Antonio Vol. II •1

The Writings of Antonio Vol. II

(Philosophical and Political Commentary)

Copyright © 2020 Antonio A. Sweeney.

All rights reserved. No part of this publication may be re-produced, distributed, or transmitted in any form or by any means, including photocopying, recording, or other elec-tronic or mechanical methods, without the prior written permission of the publisher, except in the case of brief quotations embodied in critical reviews and certain other noncommercial uses permitted by copyright law. For per-mission requests, write to the publisher, addressed "Atten-tion: Permissions Coordinator," at the address below.

All Scripture Quotations taken from The King James Ver-sion of The Bible. blueletterbible.org

ISBN: 978-1-7349934-0- (Paperback)

ISBN: 978-1-7349934-1-7 (eBook)

Library of Congress Control Number: 2020907506

This book is a work of non-fiction.

Front cover image by Artist: ColiN00B from Pixabay

Book design by Designer. Antonio A, Sweeney

Printed by Ingram Spark & KDP, USA.

First printing edition 2019.

iLearn Research And Consulting Firm

Phoenix, Arizona 85051

authorsweeney2020@gmail.com

https://www.facebook.com/antonio.sweeney.982

Dedicated To:

This book was written for mankind,

And the gods among them.

And To my Kids:

Imani, Nathan, Ophelia, and Sonia

And

to my Wife

Other Books by Antonio:

The Writings of Antonio Vol. I

(Witty, Philosophical, Political, and Sometimes Controversial Commentary on Scripture)

Contents:

Teaser

In This Book, You will Find...

- **Covenant Wisdom**
- **Creation Vs. Evolution Argument**
- **Challenge to America's Race and Class Problem**
- **Antonio's "god" Theory and mention of Principles of Eugenics**
- **Oneness Vs. Trinity Argument**
- **Biblical Spycraft**
- **Spiritual Principles**
- **Artificial Intelligence and Global Security**
- **Antonio's Theories on Societal and Global Improvement**
- **Davidic, Abrahamic, and Solomonic Wisdom**
- **Prophetic Scripture**
- **Unorthodox Solution to Middle East Problme**
- **And Much, Much More!!!**

Chapter 1

Greetings folks, well here we are another day as I finished the editing on my first book, The Writings of Antonio Vol. I, an idea of a second book came to mind. There are many commentaries on scripture out there, but I think what makes this series unique is that it presents philosophical questions, challenges the reader to examine his inward parts and thoughts or ideas about life, and God, and tackles currents; and I hope that I would continue to hear from God and His Spirit, whatever talks to me in the form of a still quite voice, or sometimes loud and clear.

A wise man once told me, that we have to be still and listen to what life is saying to US. The scripture says in a certain place to "Be still and Know, that I am God" (Psa 46:10). Yet and still, inaction for too long profits little. Once we receive instruction, it's better to carry out the command, if it is sane, or sometimes insane; who knows?

The Word that came to me this day was the scripture found in Jeremiah 31. Jeremiah was considered to be the weeping prophet to Judah, and prophesied to the people before the Babylonian captivity. He warned the people and spoke of future things. I'll record these select verses beginning at v. 31:

> Behold, the day come, sayeth the LORD, that I
> will make a new covenant with the house of Isra-
> el, and with the house of Judah: Not according
> to the covenant that I made with the fathers in

the day that I took them by the hand and brought them out of the land of Egypt; which my cove

nant they break, although I was a husband to them sayeth the LORD:

But thus shall be the Covenant that I will make with the house of Israel, I will put the law in their inward parts, and write in their hearts and will be their God and they shall be my people.

And they shall teach no every man his neighbor, and every man his brother, saying know the LORD, for they all shall know me, from the least of them to the greatest of them, saith the LORD: for I will forgive their iniquity, and I will remember their sin no more. Jeremiah 31:31-34

So, in this passage of Scripture it appears God gives Jeremiah a glimpse of the future of Judah and their spiritual standing with Himself. A few questions though: Who is the Israel of God today; the called out ones from the world, grafted into the spiritual house and receiving the benefit of the Ancient of Days with Israel. Secondly, God gives Jeremiah a foreshadowing of Christ. This text was written years before Christ physically was born and came on the scene. A mystery that he says even though they break my covenant (the commands of the law), I will put my law, Christ that is, in their inward parts, and remember their sin no more. He goes so far as to say that they all shall know me and no one will say, know the LORD.

So, God gave US his Son, or Himself, to be accepted in the hearts of mankind upon the Earth, and this seed or mystery once accepted becomes a spiri

tual law or truth, a new covenant with God in our lives and in our hearts; A new contract, that privileges the believer to a benefits package, and comes with stipulations. My challenge to you, my friend, is not to know the Lord, for you should already know Him, but discern your new covenant Oh Israel of God, what are the benefits and stipulations of your contract.

God Bless and, Have a Great Day!

Chapter 2

Greetings everyone, well another word that can inspire us and reveal a sacred mystery about our divine nature. The text comes from the gospel of St. John, out of the four gospels in the New Testament, John's testimony is considered the most philosophical. He was the youngest disciple and part of Christ's inner circle along with Peter and James. John was considered the one whom Christ loved. I can only imagine the private conversations that John and Christ had, and what spiritual knowledge he was made privy to for being close friends with Christ. I'll record the meat of the text, in which we will focus: St. John chp. 1 v. 1-3; 10-13.

In the beginning was the Word and the Word was with God and the Word was God. The same was in the beginning with God. All things were made by him: and without him was not anything made that was made.

He was in the world, and the world was made by him, and the world knew him not. He came unto his own and his own received him not. But as many as received him, to him gave he the power to become the sons of God, even to them that believe on his name.

Which were born, not of blood, nor of the will of the flesh, nor of the will of man, but of God. And the Word was made flesh, and dwelt among us, and we beheld his glory the glory of the only begotten of the father full of grace and truth. St. John. 1 v. 1-3; 10-13

Alright, so here we have sacred words of truth with the ability to change our lives and the way we perceive ourselves, others, and the world around us. Why? Because first off we find that, In the beginning was the "Word," or in the Greek, the "logos," which is the "thought" or something said; it implies reasoning, mental faculty, motive and computation. One can only think of the Genesis account of Creation where the scripture says,

In the beginning, God created the Heaven and earth, and the earth was without form and void and darkness was upon the ace of the deep. And the spirit of God moved upon the face of the waters. And God said," let there be light, and there was light. (Gen1:1-3)"

So, at the logos of God, there was creation enacted. This gives rise or support to some intelligent design. Further, while others seek proof of Creation and the beginning; Evolution and the "Big Bang Theory" go against one of the fundamental and universal principles of physics; Physics, Chemistry, Biology, Astronomy, and Geology being a few ways Scientist understand the Universe. That is, the principle that says, for every action there is an equal and opposite reaction. Creation without intelligent design; action without some external equal and opposite catalyzing force is impossible according to the very principles used to understand these things. Even when considering the law of momentum, there is an initial force involved. How do we get effect without cause? Things did not just spontaneously combust and develop into the complexity of the single brain nerve, and the inner depths of the human mind, intelligence and emotion from gasses? There had to be an intelligent mind, being, or Power behind it all; hence God.

Ok, getting back to the main point, the scripture says the Word or Logos was made flesh and dwelt among us, as the only begotten of the Father...: The thought of God, became incarnate in human flesh, what are the implications of this, the scripture says, "Lo, I come in the volume of the book, a body thou hast prepared for me" (Psalms 40:7)(Heb10:5). God's seed in the hearts of man. Listen further to what this implies to us who believe. It says, "He came to his own (the Jews of that day), but they received him not" (had him crucified)—But as many as received him(All who accept Christ), gave them the power or "exousia," that is ability, to become the sons of God. "Who were not born by the flesh, nor of blood, nor by man, but of God."

This indicates spiritual rebirth, unlike the natural birth, but much like natural birth; the inception starts with a seed of God that develops into full grown divine being inside of us, on feed from the meat, milk, and water of the Word. In the natural, the man's seed consist of 23 chromosomes of deoxyribonucleic acid or DNA, which is thought to carry genes of our phenotype, body make up, eye color, height, predisposition to illnesses and disorders. How much more if God said, let us make man in our image does His spiritual seed give us the divine ability to be like or at least imitate our Father in Heaven. We who believe and remember the Word or Christ are His offspring and progeny, have inherited certain attributes, character habits and traits.

Go find out what this means. God bless everyone and have a Great Day!

Chapter 3

Greetings this day, another Word to inspire US and to make us think of God and the principles and precepts taught by Christ concerning life here on earth for the believer and the kingdom. This day's lesson comes from the gospel of Mathew; the first of the gospels listed in the New Testament. Mathew was a Hebrew tax collector, working for the Roman government at the time of His call. He records many of the parables and sayings of Christ. Herein this passage we discover Christ speaking of what truly defiles a man, and what can be considered petty.

Essentially we find as Christ quotes from the prophet Isaiah, that it is all a matter of the heart. God cares more about the heart and what is in it, rather than the trivial things we do or left undone. Read Mathew 15 for backstory, I'll record beginning at v. 7:

"Ye hypocrites, well did Esias prophesy of you

saying,

This people draweth nigh unto me with their mouth, and honoreth me with their lips; but their heart is far from me. But in vain they do worship me, teaching for doctrines the commandments of men."

And he called the multitude, and said unto them, Hear, and Understand, Not that which goeth into the mouth defileth a man; but that which cometh out of the mouth. These defile a man. Do not ye yet understand that whatsoever entereth in at the mouth goeth into the belly, and is cast out into the drought. But these things which pro ceed out of the mouth come forth from the heart and they defile the man.

For out of the heart proceed evil thoughts, murder, adultery, fornication, thefts, false witness, and blasphemies. These are the things which defile a man but to eat with unwashen hands defileth not a man. Math. 15: 7-20.

So, Christ confronts the religious leaders of the day, or should I say responds to their attempts to back him into a corner about his disciples not washing their hands before eating. Hey, by all means, wash your hands thoroughly before eating; Surgeon General Recommended, but is this really the point. This was not the first time nor was it the last time pointing of the finger strategy was used. Christ redirected them; the religious leaders that is, to their own hypocrisy of letting the "commandments of men" break the laws of God. I begin to think of the legalism and unnecessary rules in the church that prevent or even repel people from true worship of God in Spirit and Truth. Some churches consider it unholy for women to cut their hair or prohibit them from wearing paints, or frown upon men in shorts. Some have rules of no hats in the sanctuary for men or boys or no open toe sandals for girls. Petty dress codes and rules of conduct, which are all at the surface a little harmful to the one who has not been raised in that tradition, and unware of the expectations to follow or hear a word from God, which are simply, come as you are.

Christ called these trivial things petty in so many words and says that eating with unwashed hands cannot defile a man, but what is in and proceeds from the heart. Another scripture says, "from the abundance of the heart, the mouth speaks" (Mat 12:34). So what do we prove to be in the heart of man? How did Christ know it so well, when he was said to be without sin? The scripture said he knew what was in man and therefore committed not himself to them (Jhn 2:24-25). Nevertheless, He did give and have the ultimate commitment and sacrifice for mankind, that is to release the power of his godhood and die upon the Roman Cross as a common criminal. This price he paid for what was in man, he covered the bill of murder, adultery, fornication, theft, false witness, and blasphemy at the cross. The justice system can be merciful, but murder has its sentence. Adultery can be forgiven, but in most cases hurts a marriage. His sacrifice, does not of course prevent the repercussion and earthly consequences of committing such acts;-- yet, our soul is kept by Christ when we acknowledge Him and what He did for US.

God Bless and Have a Great Day!

Chapter 4

Greetings folks, another day to shed light on truth and expose the error or correctness of our ways. To make us think of spiritual and material concepts that affects the inner life of the man. This next passage of scripture seems to paint Christ as a racist snob, but in fact he is simply challenging a women's faith and ultimately rewards her according to her belief. What if our American Race Problem was this simple. It begins in Mathew 15, I'll record starting at v. 21.

Then Jesus went thence and departed into the coast at Tyre and Sidon. And behold, a women of Canaan came out of the same coast, and cried unto him saying, Have mercy on me, Oh LORD, though Son of David, my daughter is gravely vexed with a devil.

But he answered not a word, And his disciples came and besought him, saying send her away, for she crieth after us. But he answered and said, I am not sent but to the lost sheep of the house of Israel. Then came she and worshipped Him, saying LORD help me.

It is not meet to take from the children's bred and give to the dogs. And she said Truth, Lord, but even the dogs eat of the crumbs that fill from the master's table. Then Jesus answered and said unto her, O women, great is thy faith: be it unto thee even as thy wilt and her daughter was made whole that very same hour. Mathew 15:21-28.

Alright, So—this text in and of itself present controversy; how can a loving God and Savior appear in any way racist or a bigot against another whole race of people. A darker shade of people, for the Canaanite women, more than likely was a darker shaded women, for the Canaanites descended from Ham, and Ham's decedents were thought to have migrated to the African Regions and Countries after the flood.

Anyway, first off, we see Christ responding to her first request with the ever so ominous "Silent Treatment." The scripture reads that, "He answered not a word." And when He finally did answer, He answered with an insult, calling her and her race of people dogs or second class, not human, but animals, beneath the Jews. An ordinary person would have been defeated, heartbroken for life, disabled at the miss-treatment, paralyzed by the unjust system of religiosity of the day. But this woman's tenacity caused her to respond in kind and she took on the challenge with a humble suggestion saying, that even dogs eat the crumbs from the Masters table. It's funny how Christ said it was not fair to give meat of the house to the outsiders. How well do we as Americans know of the old common complaint of supposedly "foreigners" or "immigrants" taking all the jobs—an excuse for failure or inadequacy; this may be high-minded thinking, but if we as all people view the American Race Problem as a challenge of our Faith to do better, to do best, to be rewarded according to what our faith, ability and ambition can attain, then where would we be?

Who knows—this argument only can go so far in

the face of certain Injustice, or corruption and hatred; but things are better and I believe will continue to be so. Today the poor and uneducated, disenfranchised, and depressed don't have to settle for "crumbs" or mediocrity for opportunity for success is available to all through education, the internet, free public libraries full of books, new and unique business models and the plethora of other social programs and universal helps and technologies in society. To build people up to their highest social wellbeing or order in life. So we all are left without excuse to succeed for the determined and hardworking soul who wants more and to matriculate through the social obstacles to attain their portion in life; whether it be medium, large, or small.

Which leads to the next philosophical and social question, Is the Race problem of America more a Class problem. A monetary problem that became a question of education and status. The elite and aristocracy of society will always rule over, or experience greater social well-being than the uneducated and poor; regardless of race. Or is this line of thinking also folly and will only breed hatred and resent. Simply an observation.

Hope this was motivation for all of US to do well in life, God Bless you and Have a Great Day!

Chapter 5

Good morning, afternoon, or evening friend; whichever part of the day this writing finds you in. For this session the LORD has led me a different way. Not to get too theological but there be much debate surrounding the issue of God being one God verses God being One in three persons. I am of the camp that believes scripture points to a number of instances where we see God the Father, the Son and God the Holy Spirit represented; these three being one but distinct in their identity and roles in our salvation and relationship with God. Even though no man can fully understand the depth of the Spirit and Being of God, I believe scripture gives us a clue to His person.

In the gospels and the acts a certain scripture from the psalms is quoted a few times—namely referring to the vision that King David saw of Christ and the LORD or God the Father so many years before Christ came to the earthly scene in Jerusalem. I will record this scripture along with a text from the prophetical book of Daniel speaking of the Ancient of Days and One like the Son of Man. Again we see God the Father and the Son as two distinct persons and a vision displayed to the prophet by God's Spirit, the Holy Ghost. To me, this clearly identifies God; one in three persons.

Truly this is a little off from the point Christ was trying to make in the gospel of Mathew 22: 42. He was not trying to explain the fact that He was God in three persons, but that He was Lord and before David whom the people believed to be the genealogical and patriarchal root of Christ. Listen to what Christ says to the Pharisees after multiple attempts of them trying, once again to entangle Him in doctrine. Christ says:

What think ye of Christ? Who's son is He? They say unto him, The son of David. He sayeth unto them, how doth David in Spirit call Him Lord, saying, The LORD said unto my Lord, sit though on my right hand, till I make thine enemy thine footstool? If David call him Lord, how is He his son?

And no man answered him a word, neither dust any men from that day forth ask him any more questions. Mat 22:42-46.

So, we see God in Christ had the final question of the day and shut up the sceptics and naysayers. It was obviously a supernatural power that came upon King David to allow him to see into the future or the past concerning Christ and the LORD or the Father and to hear the divine utterance of God. Secondly, remember the baptism of Christ by his cousin John. Heaven opened up, the Spirit descended upon Christ as a dove and a voice from Heaven—God the Father spoke, saying, "This is my son in whom I am well pleased, Hear Him"(Mat 17:5) I see God, the Father, the Son and the Holy Spirit in this dramatic episode of the Messiah's baptism. God the Father attended His Son's baptism, like any loving parent would do; the commencement and launching of His Kingdom Preaching ministry. Speaking of Kingdom, I will end with these verses from Daniel. Why did this Old Testament prophet by the Spirit of God see God the Father and God the Son if there only be One God in One person?

I saw in the night visions, and behold, one like the Son of Man came with the clouds of Heaven, and came to the Ancient of Days and they brought him new before him. And there was given Him dominion and glory and a Kingdom, that all people, nations, and languages should serve Him; His dominion is an everlasting dominion, which shall not pass away, and his Kingdom, that which shall not be destroyed. Daniel 7:13-14.

Chapter 6

Greetings everyone, another word to help us live and do better, this one comes from the realm of Psalm 90, a Psalm written by Moses where he highlights the Sovereignty of God in the lives of the children of Israel despite their missteps and behaviors . The Wisdom he gains and shares is necessary:

So teach us to number our days that we may apply our hearts unto wisdom.

And let the beauty of the LORD our God be upon us and establish though the work of our hands upon us yeah, the work of our hands, establish though it. Psalm 90: 12; 17.

So, any good Warrior, Business Executive, Leader, Coach, Athlete, or even student for that matter, knows the benefit of having a good strategy or plan before the battle, test, meeting, or game. I Mean, who wants to go into combat ill prepared, without a clue of what to do or what to think; taking fire, under stress and pressure, without any prior knowledge of the battlefield; or intelligence on the adversaries technology and weaponry. The field of battle can be likened to the field of life. A wise man once told me; "Know your P's, Prior Preparation, Prevents, Poor, Performance. Which simply implies that we should fore think about our lives, and livelihood and the steps it will take to get there, not to mention planning before main events. Whether it be a plan to self-actualize, make a million, or pay the rent; have a plan. Not only that, Moses asked God to teach him the number his days, that he may apply his heart to Wisdom. So while we may plan our way, we should also be learning all the while wis dom from life. Whether History, or Science, Technology and Business, Metaphysics, Philosophy and Eschatology, or Economics and the Social Sciences.

We should be becoming experts in something as we grow older and have the time to develop our knowledge and skills. Otherwise we have wasted our time hear upon the earth, and have nothing to show for our careless behavior. All the while, let us pray that God would establish the work of our hands. The proverb in psalms says, and I'm paraphrasing, "Unless God build the house, the watchmen stay up in vain"(Psa 127:1).

Hope this was helpful, Good day and God Bless!

Chapter 7

Greetings folks, yet another discussion topic from the Word, giving us insight and perspective on great questions and mysteries concerning the goings on of man and his inner life with God. Text this day comes from Genesis and focuses on Jacob's wrestling with the Angel or "Theophany," that is; a visible manifestation of God or a Deity. I'll record, and let us see what took place Herein:

And Jacob was left alone; and there wrestled a man with him until the breaking of the day. And when he saw that he prevailed not against him, he touched the hollow of his thigh; and the hollow of Jacob's thigh was out of joint, as he wrestled with him.

And he said, Let me go, for the day breaketh. And he said, I will not let thee go, except though bless me. And he said unto him, What is thigh name? And he said, Jacob. And he said, thy name shall be called no more Jacob, but Israel: for as a Prince hast though power with God and with men, and has prevailed.

And Jacob asked him, and said, Tell me I pray thee, thy name. And he said, What is it that thy dost ask after my name? And he blessed him there. And Jacob called the name of the place Peniel: for I have seen God face to face, and my life is preserved. Genesis 32:24-32.

So, we have here the story of Jacob wrestling with a "unknown man" and for purposes of this passage of commentary we are going to consider this "unknown man," God, or an idea, or even a problem in our life. I present and believe that if we hold on to God or an idea given to us by him, or even work through a problem long enough; that ultimately it often will bless US. We may come out of the tussle a little different, or even slightly touched or battered. Nevertheless, ultimately, we shall receive power with God or that idea or over that problem, and with man. Once we've gone through something or had an experience, we have gained wisdom and power over that incident. We shall even remain insightful as to how to matriculate the course if we ever were to endure it again; and further, knowledge of how to navigate the next obstacle.

Jacob had no idea of what was coming next in his life. He was to meet his long time enemy and brother and meet him with grace. He was to go his own way, and eventually endure a family, conflict of loosing a favored son; Joseph. He was to experience famine and hardship and ultimately be reunited with His son, who was Ruler in Egypt. But before these things, God said that Jacob's new name was Israel; Prince with God, having power with God and man (Gen 32:28). His name did not prevent him from hardship, but gave him power to endure it, or make it through and overcome.

That's enough for now. God Bless you friend, and have a Great

Day!

Chapter 8

Good day to you, here we are listening and taking wisdom. Today's lesson features Christ and his relationship with God, more specifically in time of trouble and when he felt furthest from Himself, or His Father. Further, we see King David prophesy by the spirit the scene of the crucifixion, using the very words Christ would use, "Father, why hast though forsaken me?" I'll record other verses in that Psalm 22, that speak to the days event that David seemingly prophesied about,--namely Christ bones not being broken, his hands and feet being pierced, and his cloths being given away by lots being drawn. What shall we then say concerning these matters; Coincidence, or Prophecy? I'll record:

My God, My God why hast thou forsaken me? Why art thou so far from helping me, and from the words of my roaring?

Many bulls have compensed me: strong bulls of Bashan have beset me round.

For dogs have compensed me: the assembly of the wicked have enclosed me: they pierced my hands and feet?

They part my garments among them, and cast lots upon my vesture. Psalm 22: v1,12,16, 18.

This prophesy Christ must have known he was to

suffer beforehand because in the garden He prayed to God saying, "Father if though be willing, remove this cup from me, nevertheless; not my will but thine be done" (Luk 22:42). Christ knew hardship. Some of us have also experienced tough times; sickness, death, accidents, judicial and litigative worries, solitude, mental breakdown, family conflict, work and financial troubles, homelessness; and all the other concerns of the day. But God is the resurrector of our situation and the one who gives us power to endure through the impossible storm. We have mastered life when we can sleep as he did in the boat while the storms rage without worry that our Father is able to calm the storm and yet keep us safe and sustain US, though water be in the boat (Mat 8:24).

The obedience that Christ displayed is hard to find in mankind; for the scripture says, He was obedient unto death, though he was God, he humbled himself as a man and endured the cross (Phl 2:8). Don't we all so quickly try to escape the hardship that seems so unnecessary. I mean, who wants to bear the cross,---really, and sacrifice the pleasure of life. He also said, I have come that they may have life, and have it more abundantly (Jhn 10:10). Some delight in living for God with Joy despite the hardship, and look for greater eternal reward. And again, who wants to live for God when you live in an evil, corrupt, and sinful society. Such was the time of Christ and his disciples in Jerusalem as they were governed by their by Rome.

God Bless a have a Great Day.

Chapter 9

Greetings Ladies and Gentlemen, this day's lesson draws attention to what man or women are capable of in desperate situations. The text shows a women in dire need of healing in her body so much so, that she didn't care for what anyone thought as she pushed through the crowd to get to Christ; her break-through and blessing. She cared not that Christ was on His way to heal another; a ruler of the Synagogue's daughter, but she insisted upon what God in the flesh could do for her condition. I'll record:

> For he had only one daughter, about twelve years of age, and she lay a dying. But as He went the people thronged Him. And a women having an issue of blood twelve years, which had spent all her living upon physicians, neither could be healed of any.
>
> Came behind Him, and touched the border of his garment: and immediately her issue of blood stanched. And Jesus said, Who touched me? When all denied, Peter and they that were with Him said, Master, the multitude throng thee and press thee, and sayest thou, Who touched me?
>
> And Jesus said, Somebody hath touched me: for I perceived that virtue is gone out of me. And when the woman saw that she was not hid, she came trembling, and falling down before him, she

declared unto him before all the people for what cause she had touched him, and how she was healed immediately.

And he said unto her, Daughter, be of good comfort: thy faith hath made the whole; go in peace. St. Luke 8:42-48.

What if we had this same mind when in need of God in our troubled situation? Not caring for what people may think or say of US, but solely concerned on what we may receive from God if we persist. This type of focus and determination takes discipline and yet balance, because it is so easy to get caught up in life, or ministry, and career and lose focus on other things such as family, health, and even finances. The world is full of politics and many people desire many things. Changes in society, changes in government, changes in the education system, the judicial system, a medical policy overhaul is needed, from the urban community to suburbia, to the rural and city life, people want and desire all kinds of things; however, as the scripture says, "God's eye's search the earth to see if he findith anyone that understands and seeks Him" (Psa 14:2).

How can we be rewarded according to our Faith, if we have none? What shall our Faith find or seek out for US in life? Surely no one wants to lose their reward from God; why won't we, or what prevents us from pressing through the crowd of life to get to Him; even like this women.

God Bless and Have a Great Day!

Chapter 10

Greetings friend, another day to think and observe our condition and meditate upon our comings and goings and interactions with others. And yet there is a benefit to the one who God separates and the one who separates himself to take time to find out what is important to oneself, life, and God. To find out knowledge of witty inventions and intermeddle with all wisdom (Pro.8:12). I'll record:

But know that the LORD hath set apart he that is godly for Himself: the LORD will hear when I call unto Him.

Through desire, a man hath, separated himself and seeketh and intermeddleth with all wisdom.

I wisdom dwell with prudence and find out knowledge of witty inventions. Psalms 4:3; Proverbs 18:1 & 8:12

So we see there is benefit for spending time alone and having solitude. Although there is nothing like the synergy that sparks in a dynamics of a group setting; we may be able to hear God more clear ly when we are alone, although he does also speak through others. The scripture tells us that God separates the godly for Himself in this Psalm written by David.

Apparently David had audience with God, for this is the reason to go to the "secret closet to pray to the Father; who rewards openly what we do and pray in secret" (Mat. 6:6). Christ often times would get away from the crowd and get alone to pray. We see even in his final hour in the Garden of Gethsemane, Christ seeking to have the cup of wrath removed from Him. This test He would have to endure for US, but was strengthened by an Angel. What witty invention shall we find out for ourselves and the world when left alone, to spend time seeking and intermedelling with all wisdom.

Go find out what this means. God Bless and Have a Great Day!.

Chapter 11

What is Truth? Is the question Pontius Pilate asked Christ when the Jewish leaders presented to Christ as one who was stirring up the population and causing trouble, sedition, and rebellion. Christ response to the challenge of the governor was so esoteric, He spoke of a Kingdom from a different World, He spoke of servants or we can assume an Army of Angels standing down, but ready to fight to deliver Him at any moment. His Kingdom was not of this world; He agreed to being called a King by the Roman Governor, but simply said He came to bear witness to the Truth. So, what is Truth today, or what is your Truth given this story and ancient document. Who hears the voice of Christ today? I'll record:

Pilate answered, Am I a Jew? Thine own nation and the chief priests have delivered thee unto me: what hast thou done?

Jesus answered, My kingdom is not of this world: if my kingdom were of this world, then would my servants fight, that I should not be delivered to the Jews: but now is my kingdom not from hence.

Pilate therefore said unto him, Art thou a king then? Jesus answered, Thou sayest that I am a king. To this end was I born, and for this cause came I into the world, that I should bear witness unto the truth. Every one that is of the truth heareth my voice.

Pilate saith unto him, What is truth? And when he had said this, he went out again unto the Jews, and saith unto them, I find in him no fault at all. St. John 18: 35-38

Would Christ and the Father be a Democrat or Republican, or even an Independent or Libertarian for that matter? Maybe he would belong to no political party at all, but his own, who knows? Does it matter? When He says, His "Kingdom is not of this world," in front of Pontius Pilot, is He implying that the true nature of Christ and God is some Alien being with a big head and large eyes like in the movies. Is that creepy or normal thinking? Who is the light and who sat beside the light to clasp hands with the son and spoke with the Father? What attracts US to the things of God and what "pheromones" do we put in the atmosphere when we sit with Him? Is it not true that mankind is attracted to light and power, the brightness of His coming shall supply all of our needs according to the knowledge He will share with US. To know Him is to have revelation of esoteric Truths that came not from men and tradition, but from God.

Have a Great Day!

Chapter 12

Greetings, I would like to talk about the time when Israel was at the Zenith of its power as a nation of people during ancient biblical times. They endured Egypt, the wilderness for 40 years, Canaan, Judges, King Saul for 40 years, King David for 40 years and all the wars, and finally reached the peak of their Power and Peace during the reign of Solomon; who also reigned for 40 years. I'll record and excerpt from Kings:

> And Judah and Israel dwelleth safely, every man under his vine and under his fig tree; from Dan even to Beersheba all the days of Solomon
>
> And God gave Solomon wisdom and understanding exceeding much, and largeness of heart, even as the sand that is on the sea shore.
>
> And Solomon's wisdom excelled the wisdom of all the children of the east country, and all the wisdom of Egypt.
>
> For he was wiser than all men; I Kings 4:25; 29-
>
> 31a

So, imagine having a 40 year stretch of peace

and blessing ona job, in a family, career, marriage. Where God gets the glory out of all that happens in your life. Some work for 20, 25, 30 years and then retire. But Solomon took the throne as a young man and reigned for 40 years with wisdom. It wasn't until, as God warned him, that one of his many strange women caused him to burn incense or worship a false god that the kingdom began to decline in his old age.

We do well to keep God as our primary interest in life, so that He will not be jealous and angry and pull down the idols of our heart until we place him in the center. For truly, stability, security, and peace in life and the afterlife ultimately come from God in whatever form that may be. Whether it be through a job, housing, family, income, business and networking, our Eternal and Temporal stability come from Him. Where are we in our lives? Are we at the Zenith and Pinnacle of our journey? Are our best days ahead? Have we plateaued? Are we still climbing to reach and attain? Are we gracefully walking down the hill; may God sustain US through our journey and may we rest well at the peak.

God Bless and Have a Great Day!

Chapter 13

Greetings everyone, what a day!? Today's lesson breeches the topic of work ethic and what a certain New Testament scripture teaches about it. Although there be many parables said by Christ, that touch on the topic, not discussed in this passage, we will approach it from a few verses in the book of Colossians; an epistle written by the Apostle Paul to the Colossian church. This letter is considered one of the Paul's jail house epistles, along with Ephesians and Philippians, and has in-depth spiritual truths that we will also consider at another time; but for now, I'll record:

> Servants, obey in all things your masters according to the flesh; not with eyes service, as men pleasers, but in singleness of heart, fearing God. Knowing that of the Lord you shall receive the reward of the inheritance, for you serve the Lord Christ. Colossians 3:22-23.

Ok, so, Paul uses the words Master and Servant and it does imply a hierarchy in the Employer, employee relationship. Who knows, I'm sure at some time even in American history this passage of scripture was used by Slave owners to justify the practice of slavery. But, I digress, what I would like to discuss here is how our work ethic, whether for a boss or ourselves should be, "as unto the Lord," who is the true rewarder of our labors. This is the principle, I think, Paul is trying to convey, that we do our work not for the sight of man, but to receive God's approval; and therefore we should be excellent in whatever we do.

The Psalm says, "Whatsoever thy hand findeth to do; do with all thy might"(Ecc 9:10a). And the Proverb says, "there is much profit in labor, but the talking of the lips leadeth to penury (Pro 14:23)." Which I interpret as saying, it doesn't matter what you do, but the attitude or spirit in which we do it in. And secondly, action is better than solely talking followed by inaction. So, let us do well in our labors whatever they may be.

God Bless, and Have a Great Day!

Chapter 14

Greetings folks, another day to learn from the scripture and attribute the right attitude and thinking to achieve the things in life we are meant to attain. Speaking of such, the Old Testament scripture in Numbers tell of a tale where 12 spies were sent to recon the land of the enemy and gain intelligence on what be there; the produce, crops, and people, their way of life. Two came back with a courageous heart to overtake the land, despite the size and force of the enemy. They figured with God, they could accomplish anything. Ultimately, Joshua was in time promoted to the next General and Spiritual Leader of Israel after the death of Moses, for as the scripture says, for his courageous heart and the fact that "another spirit" was with Him (Num 14:24). What wisdom can we take from here, and do what seems like the impossible and arduous task? If we shall not first be defeated in the mind and the heart, we have a chance of success. Listen to Joshua and Caleb's heart as the other 10 fearful spies speak:

> And they told him and said, we came into the land where thou sentest us, and surely it floweth with milk and honey and this is the fruit of it. And Caleb stilled the people before Moses, and said let us go up at once, and possess it for we are well able to overcome it.

> But the men that went up with him said we are not able to go up against the people; for they are stronger than we. And they brought up an evil

report at the land which they had searched unto the children of Israel saying, the land though we have gone to search it, is a land that eateth up the inhabitants thereof, and all the people that we saw in it are men of great stature.

And there we saw giants, the sons of Anak, which come of the giants and we were in our own sight as grasshoppers, and so we were in their sight Numbers 13 27; 30-33.

So, who can tell, maybe Joshua and Caleb were god's who had no fear of man and the other solider-spies were merely men who were logical or pragmatic. They assessed the situation and saw no recourse but to go another way besides direct warfare with this city or tribe that appeared to be greater than they in every way. Or maybe they were just fearful and had not trust and faith in God their Deliverer and Secret Weapon and Power—Elohim.

So, we see the contrast between Joshua and Caleb's heart verses the other soldier-spie's hearts. They had little faith and were focused on the impossibility of the mission or problem instead of focusing on God. They couldn't see the forest from the tree's and felt timid and small in the wake of war. Such were some of US, but we learn that a heart of courage says, we can take the land. We can accomplish the task. If God be for US, Who can be against US (Rom 8:31b). God told the people to be strong and courageous and obey His commands. This was going to be the secret to their invincibility, wealth, health, and prosperity in the future.

I think there is still some virtue, mystery and wisdom in this knowledge. The mind is where the battle starts. "If you think you can, you can..." ("If", by Rudyard Kipling), and if we defeat ourselves then only God can save US. And he has many ways of doing so. To follow up with this story and passage, the children of Israel decided to listen to the evil report and end up wondering in the desert 40 years on a journey that could and should have taken 11 days. We hope to God we can take the route of obedience and progress to our Spiritual and Material land of blessing, or "milk and honey;" or translated in today's vernacular –"oil and money, stocks and options, houses and cars; wealth and abundance, and peace with God." LOL. Or are these things also a house of cards,-- Who can tell?

Alright, God Bless and Have a Great Day.

Chapter 15

Greetings everyone, another day to taste and see that the Word is good and to learn; line upon line, precept upon precept. Yesterday chapter 43 from the book of Isaiah was in my mind, and as I read, I recognize the scripture that some Apostolic Pentecostal Churches use for the Oneness of God doctrine or argument. I do not attempt to stir up controversy here, but as we spoke on God in three persons previously, I will attempt to extrapolate the scripture here. I'll record:

Ye are my witnesses, sayeth the LORD, and my servant whom I have chosen: that ye may know and believe me, and understand that I am he: before me there is no God formed, neither shall there be after me. I even I am the LORD, and besides me there is no God formed, neither shall there be after me.

I have declared and have saved and I have shown, when there was no strange God among you: therefore ye are my witnesses saith the LORD, that I am God. Thus saith the LORD the king of Israel, and his redeemer the LORD of Hosts; I am the first, and I am the last; and beside me is no God. And who as I shall call, and shall declare it and set it in order for me, since I appointed the ancient people? And the things that are coming, and shall come, let them show unto them.

Fear ye not, neither be ye afraid have not I told

thee from that time, and have declare it? Ye are even my witnesses. Is there a God beside me? Yea there is no God, I know not any? Isaiah 43:10-13; 44:6-8.

Alright, So, God is speaking through his prophet Isaiah. The book of Isaiah, a major prophetical book of the Old Testament. It is sometimes thought to be a type of mini bible in of itself containing 66 chapters as the bible has 66 books: 39 books in the Old Testament, 27 books in the New Testament. The first 39 chapters of Isiah speak of Israel's judgments and correction; the last 27 chapters are full of redemption and contain prophecies about a Messiah.

These words in chapter 43 and 44 I believe are from Christ speaking in God through the prophet Isiah. He says he is the first and the last;--also in the book of Revelation chp. 1, Christ declares that He is the Alpha and Omega, the beginning and the end. In other words, the first and the last, the root and offspring of David (Rev 22:16).

Furthermore, the spirit of Christ or God says through Isaiah that there is no God beside Him. Well, of course he speaks to the idolatry that Israel indulged and promoted. God knew no wooden or graven image that had life. He says He was before any God formed and before there was any strange god among you. This is what God is speaking of, not that he is arguing that there Is no Son that sits beside Him. Though Christ would later say, I and the Father are One (hn 17:11) .

Isaiah spoke of the greatness of God as a mind check to every one of his day. It shows us that completely understanding God is beyond our reach. For he says, "For as the Heavens are higher than the earth, So are my ways higher than you r ways, and my thoughts higher than you thoughts" (Isa 55:9). Nevertheless, we see shadows and types of Christ, and God the Father, and Spirit throughout scripture.

Chapter 16

In the New Testament Christ does not directly speak a lot about finances, although many of his parables have a monetary or even economic premise. He does teach on giving in Luke 6:38, when he benevolently puts forward what I believe to be a universal principle of giving. I believe in the unseen realm of society and the Universe, Cosmos and in the Spirit; there be always eyes watching, and as we give unto others, the Universe, the Earth and the Spirit will return back unto US even as Christ has said. I'll record:

> Give and it shall be given unto you, good measure, pressed down, and shaken together, and running over, shall men give into your bosom, For with the same measure that ye meet, withal, it shall be measure to you again. Luke 6:38.

I will even go further and say God rewards us more than what we give, for as the old spiritual says, "You can't beat God's giving, no matter how hard you try." Other times when Christ spoke about giving, he says "let your alms be given in secret, let not your right hand know what our left hand doeth, that your fa ther who seeth in secret may reward you openly" (Mat 6:4). I have found these things to be true. God does reward us above that which we gave and do for Him.

Secondly, Christ mentions, "I desire mercy and not sacrifice," (Mat 12:7) meaning he cares more about the heart issues rather than external legal, imperfect, and even sin issues. I know this may come as a blow to the church budget, but if the hearts of God's people are right, everything will take care of itself. Tithing is good, but unnecessary for salvation, you can't buy heaven, but must believe.. I believe tithing is a faith thing that can bless the life of the believer who practices it. Do as you will, but know that God rewards Faith and Giving accordingly and even above what we have done..

God Bless and Have a Great Day!

Chapter 17

Greetings everyone, the words from today's scripture originate from the first verse in Psalm 19. They illuminate the fact that God speaks on a daily basis by and through His Creation. If we stop and listen, what are the Heavens saying? The scripture says day unto day uttereth speech. There is another verse in Proverbs that speak of knowledge crying out daily in the streets, begging the simple and the scornful to turn in to learn wisdom (Pro. 1:22). I believe this can be translated into observing the wisdom that comes from the chief places in a city. City Hall, Court rooms, libraries, Business offices of all sorts, listening to news broadcasts, not to mention the wisdom that comes from God. So we have the Wisdom that comes from God, and the Wisdom that also comes from listening to and observing man. I'll record:

Wisdom crieth without: she uttereth her voice in the streets: She crieth in the chief place of the concourse, in the opening of the gates in the city she openeth her doors saying, How long ye simple ones will you love simplicity? And scorn and delight in scorning, and fools hate knowledge. Proverbs 1:20-22.

The heavens declare the glory of God; and the firmament showeth his handiwork. Day unto day uttereth speech, and night unto night showeth knowledge. There is no speech, nor language, where their voice is not heard. There line is gone out through all the earth and their words to the end of the world, Psalm19: 1-4a.

When I think about this text, I think that there is an impetus that we should be knowledgeable in the things of God and the things of man. No man can know all things, it is said, "we know not what we should even pray for (Rom 8:26a). Nevertheless, I suggest we, as the sons and daughters of God should study politics, law, the news and court cases, and understand things of public administration and urban planning. The Psalm says, their lines go through all the earth and their words to the end of the world (19).

Does this scripture account knowingly of global politics and economics? I believe God is Omniscient and if we are to be like the Father, we should practice acquiring and accumulating knowledge of scientific, social, economic, spiritual, and even metaphysical concepts. Brother, I have a long way to go, and so many books to read. Least I forget, Solomon has said, even much learning and writing of many books is a weariness of the flesh. And with much wisdom comes grief. Further, let us not forget, not to be overly righteous. For the scripture has said there is none righteous, no not one, (Rom 3:10).

Alright, God Bless and Have a Great Day!

Chapter 18

Greetings everyone, another word that settles are proverbial spiritual stomach, food for our minds and heart, and edification for the soul. The words that were in my mind for this day's lesson was "covet to prophesy," a phrase that comes from the book of I Corinthians chp. 14. In previous chapters in this first book of Corinthians, Paul considers spiritual gifts which we learn to be divine alibies and administrations of the Spirit of God and Christ manifesting through the believer.

Prophesy is different than a Pastoral or teaching gift or office, and yet can be: revelation, knowledge, prophesy, doctrine, or interpretation. Paul encourages the mature believer to "covet" to prophesy; I wonder why he put so much emphasis on this spiritual gift.

Follow after charity, and desire spiritual gifts, but rather that ye may prophesy.

But he that prophesy, speaketh unto men to edification, and exhortation, and comfort.

But if all prophesy, and there come one that be

I

ieveth or one unlearned, he is convinced of all, he is judged of all. And thus are the secrets of his hart made manifest; and so falling down on his face he will worship God, and report that God is in you of truth.

Wherefore brethren, covet to prophesy...I Corinthians 14: 1; 3; 24-25; 39.

So, Paul tells us to covet to prophesy, the word covet in the Greek is "zeloo" and implies to have warmth or feeling for or against—affect, covet(earnestly), have (desire), move(with) envy, be jealous over, have zealously affect. I'm not sure if this is the same word that would be used for the command, "thou shalt not covet thy neighbor's wife," (Exo 20:17) but it seems fitting. Paul's word choice leads one to believe that we should be earnestly desiring to speak, or write words that foretell future events, that edify the church, and the believer. That provide insight of revelation and guidance a long our Christian journey. The Greek word that Paul uses is "propheteuo," and it connotes, to foretell events, divine, speak under inspiration, exercise the prophetic office—prophesy.

I guess the next thing to do is, to ask God, "How do we learn to prophesy?" if we are to take up this mantle.

Ok, think and meditate on these things, God Bless, and Have a Good Day!

Chapter 19

Greetings Ladies and Gentlemen, on the topic of obedience in order to gain the reward from God or obedience in order to receive what it is we are supposed to receive from God. And what is obedience but listening intelligently to the voice of Him and carrying out those holy instructions that so guide our lives.

Abraham demonstrated this a few times in His life. He first sought opportunity to have God Bless his life when he left the city of his birth where his Father and immediate family resided. All be it, he was 75 years old, he still took the leap of faith and uprooted himself and his wife and nephew and left everything he knew for a foreign land. The people he encountered in this new land may have had different culture, and different crops, even the language may have been different, but God Almighty Jehovah-Jireh was the same.

How many of US have relocated for the better and bigger blessing and breakthrough. I'll record:

Now the LORD had said unto Abram, Get thee out of thy country, and from thy kindred, and from thy father's house, unto a land that I will shew thee:

And I will make of thee a great nation, and I will bless thee, and make thy name great; and thou shalt be a blessing:.

And I will bless them that bless thee, and curse him that curseth thee: and in thee shall all families of the earth be blessed.

So Abram departed, as the LORD had spoken unto him; and Lot went with him: and Abram was seventy and five years old when he departed out of Haran.

And Abram took Sarai his wife, and Lot his brother's son, and all their substance that they had gathered, and the souls that they had gotten in Haran; and they went forth to go into the land of Canaan; and into the land of Canaan they came.

And the LORD appeared unto Abram, and said, Unto thy seed will I give this land: and there builded he an altar unto the LORD, who appeared unto him. Genesis 12: 1-5;7

What courage it took for Abraham to leave at such an old age. Years of sewing seed and planting roots in his community, and he left it all at the voice of God. It's one thing for a young man or women to leave the house their parents to go off to college, to experience life and learn some knowledge or skill for the first time, or even move out of the house and get a job. Moreover, it is another thing for the middle age man to pick up his family and kids out of school and relocate for a better job or ministry, across the country. Nevertheless, for an older man of 78 to relocate countries, and leave all, takes mighty strength, courage, power, and determination. I mean, many at that age are moving to nursing homes, and need to be cared for.

On the contrary, the rich and elderly also get to travel all the. They have fewer attachments because their children are grown, they are retired from employment, and they have nothing else to do, but tinker around the house, shop, and care for grandchildren. (smile) I'm joking. This does raise a point, perhaps the elderly do have fewer attachments, but maybe they have a culmination of community and support over the years. Regardless of the fact, what are we willing to leave, to follow the voice of God. God challenges all of US in different ways, but in many ways, Obedience eventually meets Reward and Blessing.

God Bless and Have a Great Day!

Chapter 20

Good morning friends, today we discuss the impetus Christ placed on the lives of those who desired to follow him, and how he required in them no excuse; to allow nothing, not even death of a family member, to get in the way of what Christ had for one to do. I'll record:

And another of his disciples said unto him, Lord, suffer me first to go bury my Father.

But Jesus said unto him, Follow me, and let the dead bury the ir dead. Mathew 8:21-22.

So, Christ is a very demanding commanding officer to those that wish to be his disciple and learn from his teachings. He demands commitment much like a career choice or enlistment. One may have to change locations, or select new acquaintances, or even be caused to give up some past likes or interests. This seems a little extreme and the believer is able to choose their level of commitment, but over time as one continues in the word; life begins to happen and the word slowly influences the choices in the life of the believer. Doesn't mean one can't have hobbies or things they enjoy doing, but that God begins to make Himself a priority.

Soon lifestyles are different, thinking is different, environment is different, attitudes shift;-- it is almost cultish, the way the spirit of Christ subtlety and even tually takes over one's life for the better and a more positive outlook and outcome. A new job may have training in another city and headquarters may yet be located elsewhere. The actual satellite office where one is to be employed may be in yet another location.

Such can be the likes of following Christ. We may grow from babes in one environment; receive instructions from Heaven (headquarters) to serve in another realm or satellite office. And have an itinerary of going from office to office, depending on our gifting. Some stay in one location their whole lives. I am reminded of the saying that says our lives are changed by the people we meet, the books we read, and the places we go. Let us see that we not waste our time in vain, and yet enjoy life, but that we did something with our lives toward Christ and the Kingdom of God.

God Bless and Have a Great Day!

Chapter 21

Good morning, afternoon or evening, wherever this time findeth you. Today's lesson talks about God as a God who hides himself. There is a scripture that says God is a God who "hideth himself" (Job 23:9) and further it is a glory for God to conceal a matter. Why is this the nature of the Creator of the Universe, to hide good things in Himself and hidden treasures of knowledge and wisdom in literature, science, the kosmos, and the scriptures. What makes us as humans or mankind desire to search out our destinies and purpose? Possibly because we want to understand what we are here for. We want to know what we are to receive or do from and for God. I'll record:

> It is the glory of God to conceal a thing: but the honor of kings to search out a matter. Proverbs 25:2

> Behold, I go forward but he is not there, and backward but I can not perceive him. On the left hand, where he doth work, but I cannot behold him; he hideth Himself on the right hand, that I cannot see Him. Job 23:8-9.

These verses of scripture speak of an attribute of God not mentioned very often. God, a God that likes to play hide and seek. LOL. He hideth himself, and it is the duty of mankind, kings, gods and goddess to find Him and their glory and position and task in and from Him. God places us ever so close yet apart form Him and it is our journey in life to draw nearer, to come back to him. Though the scripture say it is he that "draweth near to those who draw near to Him" (Jas 4:8). By faith and diligence; the scripture also says, "for without faith it is impossible to please Him but he is a rewarder of those who diligently seek Him" (Heb. 11:6b)

So, there is great reward in life for seeking God's face. Instances can be authenticity and blessing In family, ministry, success in career, astounding feats in society in general. It shows the person and God off to the point where it makes one think; what is their secret power? Or, it is evident that these "successful" people have at some point in their life or ongoingly "met with God," or had some type of encounter.

Christ says, "Let your good works shine before men that they may praise your Father in Heaven" (Mat 5:16)

God Bless, and Have a Great Day!

Chapter 22

Greetings again friends,--there is a scripture that says death and life are in the power of the tongue (Pro 18:21). There be those gifted in their speech and knowledge, so much so, that they know how to cut men in the heart down to size, and up for encouragement. Some have no care for what they say and are willing to say anything for provocation alone. But proverbs says be slow to speak; and to the one that holdeth his peace is considered wise (Pro 11:12). I'll record:

Answer not a fool according to his folly, lest thou also be like unto him.

Answer a fool according to his folly; lest he be wise in his own conceits. Proverbs 26:4-5

This seems to be a warning from Solomon on how to deal with foolish, loud mouthed, abrasive people, who say rude things to get under the skin so to speak. There are those beings that exist who are as such, and the wisdom from Solomon is first ignore them; Answer them not, don't let people bring you down by their foolish words. Yet on the contrary, be ready to answer a fool in a way that points to or exposes their own pride, ignorance, and foolishness. Be ready to humiliate the fool by answering him in likewise response; lest he feel like he bested a wiser man or rock higher than he. Or you can just shut up and not say anything.

Timing, wisdom, and good judgment are essential to know what to do and what to say. Let us ask of God who giveth these things freely, and with the experience of life.

God Bless and Have a Great Day!

Chapter 23

Greetings Ladies and Gentlemen; today's lesson has the subject of the "Goodness of God," Many times we ignorantly think of God as simply wrathful and vengeful and even an angry being, mad at our sins, an unrepentant Lord. And, as a matter of fact, such are some of the attributes of God; nevertheless, His love and mercy, and forgiveness,--His longsuffering and patience towards US, is what brings us salvation and life despite ourselves. I'll record a verse in Romans that describes this principle:

Or despises thou the riches of His goodness and forbearance, and longsuffering, not knowing that the goodness of God leadeth thee to repentance. Romans 2:4

So, it seems that God is eternally good and gives US enough time that we may acknowledge Him and turn from wickedness. It's like the old saying, "giving one enough rope, or leeway to hang themselves," except we as believers and unbelievers are to recognize the proverbial "extra rope" or "leeway" we've been given and swing back toward God.

This concept can be seen in many facets of life. Sometimes criminal offenders are given mercy by the judge or pardoned by high officials; and it is up to them to see what they will prove to be in society. Will they revert back to a life of criminal activity to

succeed, or will they take the legal route and of hard work and determination to claim their stake in life. Who knows, who can tell?

Other examples can be seen in the class room, College Professors give their students extra time to study for an exam. Students have one, of two options, to study harder for their test or procrastinate further by wasting time partying or on other trivial matters. I guess it depends on how gifted the student, and other factors come to mind like how well that student already knows the material and if he or she is a good test taker. But I digress, the point is, what are we going to do with the time, grace and mercy we have been given in life.

Are we not in the classroom and courtroom of life where we receive mercy and more time to study. Whatever shall we do with such precious gifts? Let us first acknowledge them.

God Bless and Have a Great Day!

Chapter 24

I do not presume to be stuck back in biblical times and drawing up scenarios that can only be understood by such scholars; But a question and the truth is; God is the same, today, yesterday, and forever. He simply reveals Himself more and more as the sagacity of time passes and history moves on. So, today's passage of scripture speaks to the protection and general relationship that God places upon our lives. Even Job was said to have a hedge or protection that the adversary scornfully and jealously asked God to remove.

In the case of Elijah and Elisha the prophets, were compassed about, ambushed, and surrounded by legions of horses of chariots sent by the king of Syria to spy out the "man of God." Elijah was said to be supposedly revealing all that was spoken in the king of Syria's bed chambers to the King of Israel; thus all Syrian king's imperialistic efforts being thwarted.

This is the faith of Elijah revealed on the protection of God to his protégé Elisha and junior prophet.

And he (Elijah) answered fear not for they that be with US are more than there that be with them.

And Elisha prayed and said LORD I pray thee, open His eyes, that he may see. And the LORD opened the eyes of the young man; and he saw: and behold, the mountain was full of horses and chariots of fire round about Elisha. 2 Kings6:16-17

So, we see that God's, Angelic, Heavenly Murderous Army of Hosts, as He is the Lord of Hosts is more than, and stronger than man's brigades. Secondly, we see that there exists a spiritual realm which is immaterial to the natural eye; a realm that cannot be seen unless the Lord open up the eye. In this realm spiritual wars take place of good verse evil. Angelic and Demonic battles of powers and principalities, maybe somewhat like some movies portray. Thankfully we know the Lord of Hosts, The Ancient of Days who is the ultimate conqueror who shall rule the nations with a rod of iron and laugh at the heathen that mock Him. He hath provision and preserve his saints

Blessed are they that know the salvation of the Lord, let them say, "Let the Lord be magnified."

God Bless and Have a Great Day!

Chapter 25

Greetings everyone, the story of when God told Abraham to offer up his son Isaac came to my mind yesterday, and I thought about it. First of all, it is a lesson on obedience to the counsel of God, Faith, and Reward. Secondly, it is a type of foreshadowing of God the Father offering his son Christ upon the cross. Thirdly, it tells of God's jealousy and how he wants pre-eminence in the heart of men. God desires the heart of man first for himself and will test us to see where we stand with Him. Thank God though He test us, He is good. I'll record:

And He said, Take now thy son, this thy only son Isaac, whom though lovest, and get thee into the land of Moriah and offer him there for a burnt offering upon one of the mountains I will tell the of.

And they came to the place which God had told him of; and Abraham built an altar there, and laid the wood in order, and bound Isaac his son, and laid him on the altar upon the wood. And Abraham stretched forth his hand, and took the knife to slay his son and the angel of the LORD called unto him out of heaven, and said, Abraham: and he said, Here am I.

And said, By myself have I sworn, saith the LORD, for because thou hast done this thing, and hast not withheld thy son, thine only son:

That in blessing I will bless thee, and in multiplying I will multiply thy seed as the stars of the heaven, and as the sand which is upon the sea shore; and thy seed shall possess the gate of his enemies; And in thy seed shall all the nations of the earth be blessed; because thou hast obeyed my voice. Genesis 22: 2; 9-12; 16-18

So, God tells Abraham to sacrifice His son,-- was He in fact showing the world through scripture what He would eventually do with Chest This is such a paradox, because the sufficing of children and offering them up to gods was a pagan and heathen practice. Who knew the One and True Living God, Yahweh would require such a commitment from one who had come from a background of pagan worshippers. Abraham was called out from among them to leave his father's house and all that he knew. But now it seems that he has been reverted back to an old and deadly systemic practice. How many of us would question and say to ourselves, "Did I really hear God?" or, "Did He really tell me to do that?"

Nevertheless, Abraham obedience revealed his heart and rewarded him greatly, as it effected the world by the blessed Christ coming through the lineage of Abraham, Isaac, and Jacob. Abraham was multiplied and died a wealthy man. It was his faith not his sight that led him, but his insight into who God was in his life.

Moreover, we see that God is jealous over his own. Though he gives us the free will, he wants us to choose obedience. As the scripture says, "Obedience is better than sacrifice." And yet, He also says, I will have mercy and not sacrifice, that forgiveness may flow when we fall short.

So, we have forgiveness as God desires mercy, but maybe we do not realize how our obedience may effect and change the world for generations to come. The Legacy that we may leave behind depending on our obedience to Him.

Something to think about.

God Bless and Have a Great Day!

Chapter 26

Greetings folks, what do you know?-- Another day to do the will of God and be led by the Spirit, yet and still we remain in our fleshly and earthly vessels, we have upon the Earth. What is our purpose? What work have we been given to do? Christ clearly knew his role, title, and work that God had provided for Him;--So much so, that it was his meat or food to do and finish. Doing the will of God fed His Spirit and gave His soul nutrition and increased His strength. Listen to what Christ says, I'll record:

In the meanwhile his disciples pressed him, saying Master, eat.

But he said unto them, "I have meat to eat that ye know not of."

Therefore said the disciples one to another, hath any man brought him ought to eat?

Jesus saith unto them, My meat is to do the will of Him that sent   me, and to finish His work. St. John 4: 31-34.

Have you ever been so involved and wrapped up in what you were doing or some project that you were working on that you forgot to eat, shower, or even consider your appearance. This is the type of passion Christ had for His work and journey. To heal the broken, and give sight to the spiritually and physically blind. Some in this generation have this type of commitment to video games. Others for school work, or high powered careers, and those with vocation, artist, actors, musicians, ministers, and business men of all kinds; --those who practice science, law and medicine, military, and public administration; being fed literally, spiritually, and figuratively by their work.

Are we so involved that it becomes meat for us to finish the project or the job. This was Christ's love for God and what he had been given to do. What work have we been given by God to do? Shall we complete it? Shall we yearn to do the will of God in our own lives as Christ yearned for his ultimate purpose, life, death, and to rise again.

Or we can take back our will and do our own thing. What would Christianity, the World and Society and Life be like if Christ had done His own thing, and just simply lived out His life as a righteous and holy man, instead of God in the Flesh who gave his life a ransom for many. Hmmm.

Who can tell?

More stuff to think about, God Bless and Have a Great Day!

Chapter 27

Greetings everybody, among the many topics discussed in this book, one of the running themes has been obedience and receiving from God in Faith whether that be following God's divine instructions or demonstrating like Joshua and Caleb, believing what God said and wanting to act in faith instead of fear. In today's passage we see the disciple and revelator John receive something from an Angel of God that will change his life. Using this scene or example of receiving from God, metaphorically speaking what it gives to us whether it be by divine messenger, or a new land, new job, ministry, a spouse, careers, or child. What is it that God wants us to seek after Him for and receive from His hand.

John had already received from God spiritual things to say and teach, concerning Christ and the life of the believer. Herein the eschatological book of Revelations we see John receiving something even more, I'll record:

And the voice which I heard from heaven spake unto me again, and said, Go and take the little book which is open in the hand of the angel which standeth upon the sea and upon the earth.

And I went unto the angel, and said unto him, Give me the little book. And he said unto me, Take it, and eat it up; and it shall make thy belly bitter, but it shall be in thy mouth sweet as honey.

And I took the little book out of the angel's hand, and ate it up; and it was in my mouth sweet as honey: and as soon as I had eaten it, my belly was bitter.

And he said unto me, Thou must prophesy again before many peoples, and nations, and tongues, and kings. Revelations 10:8-11.

What a way to be called for a second time into ministry. My question is, had the message changed? Was there more to say about Christ and the resurrection? Or, Just more people to preach to. John had been in retirement for some years, many of his colleagues had been murdered or crucified for Christ. He was some 90 years of age when he wrote the book of Revelations. And getting back to the theme which we set, he was literally receiving from the hand of God a work to do. What shall we literally receive from the hand of God? We are not all prophets, nor are we all called like John, but what blessing shall we take from the hand or an Angel at God's command, figuratively speaking. I believe God's hand is open and through Christ He shall freely give us all things, but it is our duty to find out what it shall be.

Some things to think about.

God Bless and have a Great Day!

Chapter 28

Greetings Ladies and Gentlemen. Today's scripture lesson comes again from the book of Revelations. The Greek word being apokalypsis = meaning disclosure, appearing, coming, lighten, manifestation, revealed, revelation. The passage herein discussed is found in chapter 19 verses 1=6, and describe a glorified Christ with red eyes, sword in mouth, riding upon a white horse with KING OF KINGS, AND LORDS OF LORDS written upon His vesture and thigh. This image John gives us as a pretense to a great battle between Christ and his Armies against the kings on the earth. After this battle there is judgment and then thrones set up where the people of God reign with Christ for a millennium, or 1,000 years.

> And I saw heaven opened, and behold a white horse; and he that sat upon him was called Faithful and True, and in righteousness he doth judge and make war.
>
> His eyes were as a flame of fire, and on his head

were many crowns; and he had a name written, that no man knew, but he himself.

And he was clothed with a vesture dipped in blood: and his name is called The Word of God.

And the armies which were in heaven followed him upon white horses, clothed in fine linen, white and clean.

And out of his mouth goeth a sharp sword, that with it he should smite the nations: and he shall rule them with a rod of iron: and he treadeth the winepress of the fierceness and wrath of Almighty God.

And he hath on his vesture and on his thigh a name written, KING OF KINGS, AND LORD OF LORDS. Revelations 19: 11-16

It's a unique way to think of Christianity as a "World Domination" religion. I don't presume to know all the Muslim doctrine, but the Muslim religion, Islam, has a political world domination agenda that involves enacting certain law to attempt to govern the World Powers. Not to be extreme or political, but I believe it is ultimately Christ who will reign in His Kingdom.

Rulership upon the earth is an interesting concept. How will it be set up? Will all nations be united under one King with many Kings and Lords to govern? As Christ has said to some "Well done though Good and Faithfull servant, enter though into the joy of the Lord" Mat 25:21."

Will there be meetings and parliamentary procedures followed during the millennium or will we be more divine and communicate telepathically? Will it be a global Republic or Parliament? How will this divine kingdom of God system rule the earth? Will principles of economics still be a factor? Will man still labor? I guess some of this will be quite unnecessary because we will be in spiritual form, those who pass into the afterlife with Christ. How do the Angels of God fit into the hierarchy? Christ said, "when we shall rise, they are not married and given in marriage, but are as the Angels" (Mar 12:25). Interesting and fascinating things to think upon and consider!

God Bless and Have a Great Day!

Chapter 29

Greetings everyone, in the story of Daniel, he and his three friends are taken captive by King Nebuchadnezzar and the Babylonian Empire as first prophesied by the prophet Jeremiah, that Jerusalem would be under siege by the Babylonian foreign power. Nevertheless, Daniel and his three friends were given favor to stand in the Kings courts because of their uncommon wisdom and knowledge and ability to learn and understand science, literature, and the language of the Chaldeans.

Not to mention Daniel had understanding of all dreams and visions; much like Joseph, a gift that would aide him in promotion to prime minister and enthrall him in the journey of dreams consisting of Heavenly hierarchy being revealed and World powers and politics unfolding.. God was gracious in the wisdom bestowed upon Daniel, so much so, that it threatened and rewarded His life because of Daniel's faithfulness to God above all earthly governing authorities, including Kings.

In the passages of scripture we will simply highlight the supreme gifting and ability of Daniel and his three friends and use _their_ example of intellect for inspiration and motivation to aspire to higher things. Shall we not also desire to have these abilities and skills in acquiring knowledge of Literature, Science, Language, Cosmology, God, and History, not to mention Government and Economics. I'll record.

Children in whom was no blemish, but well favored, and skillful in all wisdom, and cunning in knowledge, and understanding science, and such as had ability in them to stand in the king's palace, and whom they might teach the learning and the tongue of the Chaldeans.

As for these four children, God gave them knowledge and skill in all learning and wisdom: and Daniel had understanding in all visions and dreams. Daniel 1: 4 & 17.

So, Daniel and his three friends were ivy league equivalent in aptitude and intelligence. They were science, language, majors of Ancient Wisdom, they had knowledge of astrology, and were taught Babylonian public administration. What about Daniel and his three friends Hananiah, Mishael, and Azariah, can influence us toward educating ourselves more;-- it was said they were ten times better than their Babylonian piers. Not that we take on an attitude of extreme competition, but seek how God's knowledge, wisdom, and divine gifting can aid in social upward mobility. This can be the answer to poverty, this can be the solution to help turn ghettos into smart cities.

What if we changed our culture to a smart culture where kids aspired to study wisdom and seek the mysteries of God as opposed to droning out on video games and young adults wasting time on drug use and alcohol addiction; defeating themselves with fatal substance abuse. What else can lift our nation, so that we can be known not only as a military, and industrial-technological, economic superpower in the world, but also that our Race of "American People" be known as enlightened, insightful, intelligent, and wise. That this be the stereotype of the every American citizen and that we not be known as "stupid or dumb, insensitive Americans" around the world. Although, there is obvious need for the "stupid and dumb, insensitive American" (smile).

Just an idea and a thought, we can call it the Divine Knowledge Revolution, seeking God and His Wisdom for Social upward mobility. LOL. The caveat being that this divine knowledge is not only biblical or supernatural knowledge, but that it challenges every citizen to become expert. It challenges every global citizen to strive for excellence and not mediocrity, weather Asian, Latino, Black, White, Middle Eastern, or otherwise. This may be idealistic thinking, but I believe it can help as a contribution to the betterment of US, and Everyone for that matter, as a culture and people. That we all become better equipped. This would drive down crime, cleanup ignorant attitudes by way of the knowledge of History and Theory. Hopefully this thing catches on. Man, once again, do I have a long way to go.

Some things to think about.

God Bless and Have a Great Day!

Chapter 30

Greetings everyone,--today's lesson is a bit of challenge for me, I'm not sure why, but it regards the believer as a nation of priest and peculiar people. From the old testament, God's peculiar treasure of priests in the Earth. A Kingdom of priests and Kings, because of God's word. What a notion this could be if taken seriously. If every believer took on the office of priest and saw themselves as a servant ruler of God, what would society and the world benefit, how would the world change? Not that we all become prudes, self-righteous , and arrogant, but that we all know God and His will. Would business and commerce be different? Principles of economics and world politics influenced by an ingrown kingdom of priests ruling in society.

Some may immediately go to the argument of "separation of church and state", and though this be the spirit of the law of the first amendment according to Thomas Jefferson, we see that many civilized and governing officials still carry their faith to the political marketplace which is acceptable. I am not suggesting that the Priest influence the President, but that the President himself, be a Christian Priestly fellow, peculiar in his habits, able to administrate justice and war matters in foreign policies, but not neglecting diplomatic measures to secure our borders and benefit our economy, lifting our nation. Maybe these are thoughts too high for me, a priestly scoundrel, but I do presume to prophesy a kingdom of God coming. Crazy I know, and yet I know not as I am known. I'll record:

> Now therefore, if ye will obey my voice indeed, and keep my covenant, then ye shall be a peculiar treasure unto me above all people: for all the earth is mine:
>
> And ye shall be unto me a kingdom of priests, and a holy nation. These are the words which thou shalt speak unto the children of Israel. Exodus 19:5-6
>
> But ye are a chosen generation, a royal priesthood, an holy nation, a peculiar people; that ye should shew forth the praises of him who hath called you out of darkness into his marvelous light 1 Peter 2:9

So, there be a lot mentioned in these passages of scripture, but the running theme is the peculiar priesthood. In Exodus and the New Testament seems that this idea would have some effect on the world and world events. That first the scripture says the mystery of iniquity will be revealed, pointing to a man of sin. Who knows if the mystery of righteousness is the kingdom of God that is supposed to rule in the millennium after the return of a glorified Christ.

What should we look for in the earth, and politics and the daily news of current events that we may be awake and vigilant? Possibly we should look to intelligently listen to the voice of God that we may be discerning of the "signs of the times". Christ himself said and I paraphrase, "you are able to discern the face of the sky, but do not know the sings of the times" (Mat 16:3). To discern we need knowledge of the scripture, specifically prophesy, spiritual knowledge, knowledge of history and current events.

Happy Studying to All of US.

God Bless and Have a Great Day!

Chapter 31

Greetings everyone, today's lesson briefly covers the topic of pride, false humility, and letting one's works shine before man as Christ implied during his Sermon on the Mount message as He gave the parable or analogy of good works being likened to a candle on a candlestick. It is what one does with this candle of good works that will either give light to the whole house, or because of false humility be hid under a bushel. This can be confusing because Christ also talks about doing things such as giving and praying to God in secret that God may reward us openly. But when it comes to good works, Christ does not want us to hide in false humility, but be the proud doer and show off the praise of God, bringing light to the world.

> Ye are the light of the world. A city that is set on an hill cannot be hid.
>
> Neither do men light a candle, and put it under a bushel, but on a candlestick; and it giveth light unto all that are in the house.
>
> Let your light so shine before men, that they may see your good works, and glorify your Father which is in heaven. Mathew 5:14-17.

So, just being real, who really wants to be a show off all the time? Humility does have its place in the Christian life. One should not be boasting about cars and the amount of money in their bank accounts, but then again, if one has been tremendously blessed by God in that capacity is Christ saying that He wants one to show off their fleet of vehicles and how God has prospered their revenues in business? I think so. So discretion and discernment is needed to distinguish between pride, showing off the goodness of God, and false humility.

Hiding God's works all together would be one who never give tribute or testimony to what God has done or allowed in one's life. Never sharing how God brought you through that fiery trial of life, never posing of Facebook (LOL), and never being one to stand and say how Good God has been. This is in a different context, but one verse says, and I paraphrase the words of Christ, "he that confess me before man in this sinful generation, I will likewise confess Him before my Father and His Holy Angels; and He that denieth me before man, I will likewise deny before my Father and His Angels),Mat. 8L38)."

God Bless and Have a Great Day!

Chapter 32

Greetings folks, today we talk a little bit about the adversary, and his occupation upon the earth and how he attempts to challenge God, and His authority and His people. In the first chapter of the book of Job, we see Satan; when Ezekiel and Isaiah describes him, they describes him as the anointed cherub that covers (Eze 28:14), cast down from the stars of Heaven, (Lucifer, how are thou fallen? (Isa 14:12), to the earth and to hell the pit. Satan made the mistake of saying in his heart that "I will be as God, and exalt my throne above the stars of heaven; I will be like the Most High" (Isa 14:13-14). Fortunately, He was sadly and poorly mistaken.

Nevertheless, we see in Job, the Devil crashing a meeting between the sons of God and God as they presented themselves, he came "as a roaring lion, walking to and fro throughout the earth seeking whom he may devour" (1Pe 5:8). This "roaring lion" part is a description used by Peter in the New Testament, and there is only One True Roaring Lion and that is Christ the Lion from the tribe of Judah, the root and offspring of David. And Christ said about the devil, that he only comes but to kill, steal, and destroy, but I have come(Chrst) to give life and life more abundantly (Jhn. 10:10b), Satan is described as and seen as a preda tor upon the sons and daughters of God, and "Devil" is interpreted as accuser or slander of the brethren. Satan implies arch enemy of God or one who opposes God. Ironically the devil's first Angelic name; Lucifer, means "light bearer."

Back to Job, God asked Satan, "Whence cometh thou?" even as He asked Cain, in the book of Genesis after he had slain his brother Able, "What hath thou done?" (Gen 4:10). We see that God asks mankind as well as His created Angelic beings a question at the suspicion of evil. Even in the garden of Eden when Adam and Eve after eating the forbidden fruit from the tree of knowledge of good and evil, The Lord walked in the garden in the cool of the day and asked Adam "Where art thou?" (Gen 3:9). Now we know that God is Omniscient or All Knowing and discerns and sees through all things. He Knows the answer before we were born or even conceived but He confronts His created beings with the opportunity to be honest with themselves and their Maker.

And usually, as recorded in Scripture, the created being is honestly answers the Most High, except in the case where the three divine beings visited Abraham and Sarah. Abrahams and his wife were over the age of 90 when being promised by God to have a son, and Sarah laughed. The theophany said, "Why did though laugh?", yet she denied, and He said, because of this, you shall have a son (Gen 18:13)(Gen 18:10).. We find that Abraham and Sarah's son Isaac was named by God, and his name Isaac, has name meaning "laughter."

Bringing the discussion forward to Christ, and forgetting the adversary for now, remember the women at the well, Christ asked where was her husband, and she said she had none. Thus Christ said she answered truly having had five that were not her husbands, including the one she currently had. So Christ took on the nature of God, His own nature, thus confronting man with hard questions to answer for some. Christ asked his disciples." Who do men say that I am?" (Mat 16:15?). In another place, "Do you believe I am able to do this?" (Mat 9:28b).

What question is God in Christ asking, confronting, or challenging you with today? How will we respond to our Maker? Some things to think about.

God Bless and Have a Great Day!

Chapter 33

Solomon is one of my favorite characters of the Old Testament. I really enjoy Proverbs and Ecclesiastics and how Solomon prayed for wisdom, judgment, and an understanding heart as a young man as he began to take the throne. I like how God blessed him with a full heart, experience and how he sought out to know and understand mankind and God in various phases of life. I call him the first Father of Psychology and a Great Philosopher. I shouldn't say this, but I also always admired how he had 700 wives and 300 concubines and wondered how he did it, and what was the nature of the relationships with these many women. How many were simply political arrangements, and how many were romantic? How many kids did he really have? Makes me wonder was Solomon the Ancient of Day pornographer, but I digress. In Ecclesiastes, we see part of Solomon's thesis for life, I'll record:

I, the Preacher was King over Israel in Jerusalem. And I gave my heart to seek and search out by wisdom concerning all things that are done under heaven: this sore travail hath God given to the sons of man to be exercised therewith.

I have seen all the works that are done under the sun; and, behold, all is vanity and vexation of spirit.

That which is crooked cannot be made straight: and that which is wanting cannot be numbered.

I communed with mine own heart, saying, Lo, I am come to great estate, and have gotten more wisdom than all they that have been before me in Jerusalem: yea, my heart had great experience of wisdom and knowledge.

And I gave my heart to know wisdom, and to know madness and folly: I perceived that this also is vexation of spirit.

For in much wisdom is much grief: and he that increaseth knowledge increases sorrow. Ecclesiastes1: 12-18

In my interpretation, Solomon learned all the rules and what it meant to be one who follows them. Then discovered what it meant to break some of them and understand some things from the madness and folly perspective. He drank wine, he knew women, he knew labors and construction, wisdom, knowledge, and song, principles of business, economics, government, and he knew God. In the end he said , God would bring everything into judgment, every secret thing, weather good or evil (Ecc 12:14). Thank God for His mercy in Christ. And Christ has said, "A greater than Solomon is here" (Mat 12:42).

So, what does this mean for US today or what wisdom can we pull from Solomon's life. Well, we see that Solomon understood his purpose for being upon the Earth. He was to gain skill in learning; knowledge, wisdom, understading many things about man and life and relay it back for a legacy and for generations to come. Of course he did more than this, but isn't that what the greatest of men have done; written down their discovery, research, findings, inventions, documented their revenue stream, financial strategy, recorded war histories, and their inner most philosophic thoughts for the evolution and development of mankind and to leave their contribution and legacy behind.

So, what will be yours? Your life work, mission statement, contribution to the world, and society; what did you learn and find out while living upon the earth? Surely you have gained some wisdom from life about your fellow man and the Universe if you have payed attention. What will your legacy be? Some things to Ponder.

God Bless and Have a Great Day!

Chapter 34

Greetings everyone, in today's lesson Paul refers to the scripture in Psalms that says, "There is none righteous, no, not one." The passage goes on to describe how there are none that understand or seek God, and all have gone their own way. Today man has ventured off into many endeavors and accomplished many things. Many, including those that sit in churches have placed their travails of life before God.—and yet, there are those that truly take time out to think upon and seek the face of their Creator.

Christ has said, "no one is good, but God" (Mar 10:18) and in another place Christ said, "if you being evil know how to give your children good gifts, how much more God the Father give good gifts to those who ask Him" (Luk 11:13). So, the overall consensus is that only God is without sin and holy and his Creation mankind is evil and full of fault. But Christ came to redeem US, and we would not then know sin unless we had knowledge of God's laws. God's laws make us aware of the sin in our lives and shows us our evil.

This is the reason why some of US choose not to read the scriptures or certain parts that point at US and laugh and mock our misbehavior with threats of missing paradise and hell fire. But if we keep reading and embrace the truth, we find God's unconditional love and mercy, forgiveness, mercy, and blessing. I think that God does have a sense of humor.

As it is written, There is none righteous, no, not one: There is none that understandeth, there is

none that seeketh after God.

They are all gone out of the way, they are together become unprofitable; there is none that doeth good, no, not one. Romans 3:10-12

Alright, I do really consider what Paul realized from the Psalms and what Christ said about the reality of man. Some humanists believe that the innate nature of man is good. But according to biblical principle, natural man is evil, "the heart is exceeding wicked and who can know it" (Jer. 17:9). This is why a savior is needed to redeem man from his natural fallen state. Many a men's natural tendency is to fornicate and many struggle with anger, and can be violent at times. But temperance is taught by God. God, I do believe has a sense of humor and gives his children gifts.

In whatever moral state we find ourselves in, I believe we should attempt to seek and know God for oneself personally, and then who can judge God's servant but God.

God Bless and Have a Great Day!

Chapter 35

Greetings everyone, today we are discussing the idea of the foreknowledge of God and predestination. While some theologians have breached the topic such as Calvin, as he talks about predestination and salvation, we will herein refer to scripture in Ephesians and Jeremiah and think about what it means to be pre-known and chosen for inheritance in God. The scripture talks about how God and Christ blessed us with spiritual blessing in heavenly places before the foundation of the world. That means before he formed the world, as he knew of the redemptive plan and coming of Christ He also knew each of us whom he adopted as children or sons and daughters by way of Christ.

It was God's own counsel that created this carnal mind of mankind and His plans cannot be changed. Who can disturb the plans of God? So, if He chose us for an inheritance in Heaven unto Himself, you'd be sure to believe that no one can steal it from Him. Shall not God guard his inheritance with an arsenal of Heavenly and Divine Hosts? You'd think that this would prevent us who believe from going through trials, but maybe the trial itself is our protection as we come forth as gold, precious metals, and good things. I'll record in Ephesians:

Blessed be the God and Father of our Lord Je

sus Christ, who hath blessed us with all spiritual blessings in heavenly places in Christ:

According as he hath chosen us in him before the foundation of the world, that we should be holy and without blame before him in love:

Having predestinated us unto the adoption of children by Jesus Christ to himself, according to the good pleasure of his will,

In whom also we have obtained an inheritance, being predestinated according to the purpose of him who worketh all things after the counsel of his own will: Ephesians 1:3-5; 11

I guess the only way we could understand the pre-selection of God is through the study of eugenics. From man's prospective the practice of eugenics would be similar to God having foreknowledge of those he chose for his heavenly inheritance. Eugenics is the human breeding for better genetic gene adoption to deter human genotype from certain genetic diseases and conditions. In God's predetermination, it is not in breeding but creating;--the very knowledge of all the ramifications that our genetic makeup may have; despite our human imperfection, he still foreordained us not only for salvation, but in blessing our earthly journey as well.

The counsel of God does all of this without taking away our free will because the power of his knowledge knows what we will choose before we select our next step. It's like those "choose your own destination" books, except God knows the path to each ending. The controversy behind this idea of pre-selection or predestination is what about the ones God did not select for salvation, why would a loving God create or foreknow some for dishonor or eternal destruc-tion. As it is said in the scripture, who can say to the Maker, "why has thou made me thus way"(Isa 63:17)? But, on the contrary, maybe we can ask, and get an answer from God. We all have free will to choose to believe for salvation, so, there is no excuse.

God Bless and have a Great Day!

Chapter 36

Greetings everyone, today's lesson comes from the prophetic book of Daniel. In Daniel, among many things, it talks about King Nebuchadnezzar as King of Babylon, (which today is modern day Iraq) as a glorious and Conquering nation of gold. One of the first visions that Daniel interpreted for Nebuchadnezzar, the king built a stature of himself for it represented His powerful kingdom and the next 3 kingdoms to rule the Ancient World after Him. According to the book, God saw pride in Nebuchadnezzar and decided to give him another dream where a tall tree was cut down to a stump and the heart of a man exchanged for a beast. Daniel later interpreted the dream to mean that God was going to bring Nebachadnezener low for seven seasons until he acknowledged the fact that God rules in the heavens and giveth the kingdom to whomsoever he chooses. I'l record.

Let his heart be changed from man's, and let a beast's heart be given unto him; and let seven times pass over him.

This matter is by the decree of the watchers, and the demand by the word of the holy ones: to the intent that the living may know that the most High ruleth in the kingdom of men, and giveth it to whomsoever he will, and setteth up over it the basest of men.

This is the interpretation, O king, and this is the decree of the most High, which is come upon my lord the king:

That they shall drive thee from men, and thy dwelling shall be with the beasts of the field, and they shall make thee to eat grass as oxen, and they shall wet thee with the dew of heaven, and seven times shall pass over thee, till thou know that the most High ruleth in the kingdom of men, and giveth it to whomsoever he will.

And whereas they commanded to leave the stump of the tree roots; thy kingdom shall be sure unto thee, after that thou shalt have known that the heavens do rule.

At the same time my reason returned unto me; and for the glory of my kingdom, mine honor and brightness returned unto me; and my counsellors and my lords sought unto me; and I was established in my kingdom, and excellent majesty was added unto me.

Now I Nebuchadnezzar praise and extol and honor the King of heaven, all whose works are truth, and his ways judgment: and those that walk in pride he is able to abase. Daniel 4:16-17; 24-26; 36-37.

I think one of the running themes in this book and these passages, is that God rules not only in the heavens, but also in the kingdom of man, to the point t\hat he sets whoever he wills up. Even the beast of men. The other warning is that God can always humble us as well. In short, it is God that is Sovran in the nations whether it be Ancient Babylon(Iraq), Jerusalem, Media Persia(Iran), Greece, Rome, the Far East, Latin America or the Good ole USA.

What's interesting is that the ancient Iraqi king gave honor to the king of Heaven and the Most High in order to be restored to his place and ruling office. It was his pride that brought him low as he said, "Is it not I that built Babylon for my glory and majesty?" The proverb says "pride goeth before destruction" and "these seven things doth God hate," pride being one of them, and yet He loveth the "proud doer of the work".

Moreover and Further, is it not interesting that Ancient Babylon or Iraq's king is in the bible giving honor to the Jewish God, not Allah. This begs the question who was the first supreme God in Iraq or Ancient Babylon. Was it God the Most High-Yahweh or Allah the god with the name taken from the moon deity.

Some things to think about.

God Bless and Have a Great Day!

Chapter 37

Greetings Folks,--in today's passage of scripture, we see excerpts from a contest between the
One and True living God of Elijah, and the prophets of
Baal at Mount Carmel. This story shows the drastic
means that pagan prophets will go through in order to
get a response from their god. The prophets of Baal
cut themselves, jumped up and down, screamed and
yelled, all for nothing; no supernatural move. In other
places they are known to offer up human sacrifices to
bless their god. How ironic that Christ becomes the
eternal, sinless human sacrifice, being God incarnate,
no more need for this practice thereafter this great
act.

On the other hand, Elijah gave himself a hand-
icap by pouring water on the wood and bulluch and
God, the Loving, yet Vengeful God of Abraham, Isaac,
and Jacob lapped up the alter and the water with a
pillar of fire from Heaven. A Supernatural move from
God happened that could not be denied. God was put
to the test and passed not by trial and error, but with
flying colors. I'll record verses from the event:

And Elijah came unto all the people, and said,
How long halt ye between two opinions? if the
LORD be God, follow him: but if Baal, then follow

him. And the people answered him not a word.

And it came to pass at noon, that Elijah mocked them, and said, Cry aloud: for he is a god; either he is talking, or he is pursuing, or he is in a journey, or peradventure he sleepeth, and must be awaked.

Hear me, O LORD, hear me, that this people may know that thou art the LORD God, and that thou hast turned their heart back again.

The fire of the LORD fell, and consumed the burnt sacrifice, and the wood, and the stones, and the dust, and licked up the water that was in the trench.

And when all the people saw it, they fell on their faces: and they said, The LORD, he is the God; the LORD, he is the God. 1 Kings 18: 22; 27; 37-39.

This comedic scene recorded in the book of 1 Kings is simple yet powerful. We see the ability of God's prophet to humbly command the arm of God for His(God's) Glory. Somewhere in scripture it talks about the Lord's servant will do great exploits (Dan 11:32b). Interestingly enough, the bible acknowledges the power of evil as well. Although it does not trump Almighty God, even today there be those that practice certain occult practices and even conjure magic spells, various forms of sadism. But for those that follow and trust God, thier spirits and souls are protected from this castigation.

Have you ever been subject to the other side of some dark spell, evil eye, demonic attack, or bad prophesy? The power and Spirt of Almighty God is how we overcome darkness. For we wrestle not against flesh and blood, but against powers and principalities that war against the soul (Eph 6:12). Therefore we have the amour and weaponry of God. God's words transact preeminence.

God Bless and Have a Great Day!

Chapter 38

Greetings Ladies and Gentlemen, the selected verses in this discussion highlight the topic of how men should strive to be wealthy according to the wisdom from the scripture. This may be seen as an old topic for a Christian disciple, but I believe that following God comes with blessing and that God is able to establish His people. This particular scripture talks about Boaz being a mighty man of wealth. Many of God's men were ultimately and eventually wealthy. Abraham, Isaac, Jacob, Joseph, Daniel, Solomon, Josiah, Hezekiah, to name a few from the Old Testament.

Of course things were a bit different in the New Testament with the first century Christians, yet and still, Christ taught many verses on the ultimate blessing on following him such as, He came to give life and life more abundantly, and the hundredfold blessing that comes with leaving all to follow Him. I have found that these blessings come with time and over years of following God. Some may have different experiences, but Wisdom has been a slow teacher for me and understanding takes time.

And In reality, if any individual keep pressing forward and diligently follow the voice of God and Christ, they will eventually amount to a peculiar and unique individual, there should be something special about their life that causes them to be blessed.

Whether it be what they have committed to do, or otherwise. Moreover, anyone who sticks with any good thing that can be profitable long enough, may see a good return. I'll record in Ruth:

And Naomi had a kinsman of her husband's, a mighty man of wealth, of the family of Elimelech; and his name was Boaz. Ruth 2:1

So, in brevity, Boaz was a mighty man of wealth, and gained a wife being the kinsmen redeemer of Ruth. Now that kinsmen Redeemer phrase is a theologically loaded phrase that can be discussed in another format, but the main point that Boaz was legally and by right the next of kin to take Ruth to wife. Boaz was a man of wealth, and good things come to men of wealth. I'm reminded of the parable, where Christ teaches, "He that hath to him more shall be given, and he that hath not, what he hat shall be taken away"(Mat 13:12). Now Christ was talking about talents and ability and rewarded those that multiplied what they had been given and scolded those who hid what they had by making no effort to profit. Of course this my fly in the face of economic policy that tries to lift those of us that have incomes below the national poverty line, yet and still, it's a spiritual and universal principle taught by God. Truly the rich get richer and the gap between rich and poor widens.

The question Is, what does it take to become a

man or women of means, substance and wealth. God doesn't just supernaturally bless us with money from the sky, at least not all the time, and money doesn't grow on trees, unless you're cutting them down, or selling them or something like that. Is it holding a good job, is it starting a business, investing in stocks, benefiting from an inheritance and insurance, investing in stocks, bonds, options, commodities, real estate, oil, or the foreign exchange; writing a book, becoming and expert academically or vocationally;-- which path is it?

The proverb says strong men retain riches, and money answereth all things (Pro 11:16)(Ecc. 10:19). This does not make money a God, but that money is a tool and resource that we can use and that enables us to do all that we want and need to do, for the Kingdom or otherwise. Money can bring happiness but not ultimate salvation. Let us pray that God show us the path to wealth and add no sorrow to it (Pro 10:22). Such is the blessing of God.

God Bless and have a Great Day!

Chapter 39

Greetings everyone;--the scripture lesson to-day points to the fact that God is a God who answers prayer. This is seen multiple times in the bible and maybe some of you have experienced this phenomenon personally, but the challenge comes to the decision we all have to make in what will we ask for ourselves when we know that God answers prayer? We have many examples in the bible of men and women beseeching God. Jabez is a man we know little about except that he falls in the lineage of David and Christ and out of a list of names, the bible records Jabez as one who prayed a simple prayer and that God granted his request.

God granted the request of many in the Old and New Testament. Solomon prayed for Wisdom, David prayed for success in battle, Joseph and Daniel prayed to interpret dreams at the request of a head of state, Samson prayed for end of life strength. In the New Testament , when Christ comes on the scene, he is often recorded saying, according to your faith, and as you have believed, so be it unto you. Another Psalms says, as a man thinketh in his heart, so is he (Pro 23:7). So what will we ask an Almighty Sovereign God. I'll record:

And Jabez called on the God of Israel, saying, Oh that thou wouldest bless me indeed, and enlarge my coast, and that thine hand might be with me, and that thou wouldest keep me from evil, that it may not grieve me! And God granted him that which he requested. 1 Chronicles 4:10.

What should we ask God for, really? On a global level, maybe world peace and that his kingdom would come, that it would be done on Earth as it is in Heaven. On a National and Local level that our cities and states would prosper. On a personal level, we pray for our necessities, and ask God that He would generally bless our lives, family, and occupations. But when it comes to that big thing that we get to ask God, and I'm not talking about a healing or new car, but to be blessed to give away cars, or for a gift of miracles that allows us the witness the power of God's healing in other peoples lives. What big thing should we ask for? To know God more intimately? To write Pulitzer prize, thought provoking books, for extreme success in business, extreme spiritual ability in acquiring wisdom and knowledge, to prophesy, that our offspring are safe and develop into who they are supposed to be? What is it?

How about to know what our Maker created US for, to know His purpose and will for our lives and accept it with peace. Who knows, but let us all seek to understand that God is able to grant our request and let us think hard about what we shall ask the Father. For it has been said, "eye hath not seen, nor ear heard, neither entered into the heart of man, what God has prepared for those who love Him" (1Co 2:9),

Further, Christ has said, "ask and it shall be given, seek and ye

shall find, knock and it will be open unto you (Luk" 11:9).

What will we do with this potential power?

God Bless and Have a Great Day!

Chapter 40

Greetings Ladies and Gentlemen, recorded in the gospels Christ taught his disciples how to pray, by giving them the example that we call, "The Lord's Prayer." The Lord's Prayer has some elements included in it that covers the basic necessities as well as eschewing one from evil. This basic prayer asks for the will of God to be done, in the life of the believer. What if everyone began to pray as a first order of business in the morning? What does the World and family begin to look like when all men pray for the will of God? Maybe this is dreaming for some Utopian Society that still is in itself imperfect and in the need of a reality that people can withstand. However, given the present consensus, it doesn't look like we will be getting there anytime soon. But all men should still pray. I'll record a few verses:

And it came to pass, that, as he was praying in a certain place, when he ceased, one of his disciples said unto him, Lord, teach us to pray, as John also taught his disciples.

And he said unto them, When ye pray, say, Our Father which art in heaven, Hallowed be thy name. Thy kingdom come. Thy will be done, as in heaven, so in earth.

Give us day by day our daily bread

And forgive us our sins; for we also forgive every one that is indebted to us. And lead us not into temptation; but deliver us from evil. Luke 11:1-4.

So, we see Christ teaches his followers how to pray and strength comes from first knowing where God is,==Heaven. And that His will is to bring Heaven to Earth. We see forgiveness, mercy, and a petition that God would not lead us astray into darkness, but as Said somewhere else. that we would be the light. In the real world, people prefer not to be exposed to the light but want to hide in darkness. For the scripture says, "they loved darkness because their deeds were evil." No one wants to have all their immoral peccadilloes exposed publically, that can be quite humiliating. Nevertheless, Thank God for boldness of heart to stand for what one believes in despite the frowns of society.

Not to mention new and upcoming technology or should I say old technology used by the Department of Homeland Security and Some local Police Departments in some cities across the country where Artificial Intelligence has exponentially heightened the effectiveness of the surveillance camera. You would be amazed at the processing and analytical capability that what would seem an ordinary camera could do these days with the assistance of AI. Pretty soon, we will be in a *1984* state where "Big Brother" is always watching or listening, our every move for protection against terror and crime, or is it the inception of control and fear?

During the Obama Admiration, not that I'm a political buff by any means, but it was an error of transparency, even certain elements of the CIA were exposed. During Bush's administration there was the Patriate Act, where conversations could be listened to without federal warrant. And now during Trump's administration we have the Data collection minefield of Jeff Bezoz Amazon with products such as Alexa that listen to conversations in our homes. I mean, don't get me wrong, I'm all for AWS support and hope to even become certified. I'm just stating the facts. Audio Google recordings and browser search monitoring on our cell phones and computers.

And So, maybe what Christ said is only partially true or only to a certain extent, because maybe some men love darkness not because the deeds where wicked, but because some secrets need to be kept. Elements of National Security and domestic precautions have to be kept under lock and key if not anything else but for having an edge, leverage, and element of surprise over and against the enemy. Alright, I'm simply and enthusiast.

God Bless and have a Great Day!

Chapter 41

Greetings Ladies and Gentlemen, today's thoughts stem from an Old Testament passage in the major prophetical book of Isaiah. It is a scripture we often hear during Christmas the in churches and who knows, maybe some synagogue's. It points to the birth of the Messiah, in so many words, the fact of Him being God incarnate and having the government upon his shoulders. Wonderful, Counselor, he is called Almighty, and Prince of Peace. I take these very descriptive names to mean He is a Sovereign miracle worker, imbued with all wisdom and Power even unto himself and to the nations.

Who can withstand His might? Yet God gracioOuslly calls us forward, to set beneath his hand of instruction and we shall live a Life of wonder as we are captivated by His work in our lives. For the scripture says, "we are his workmanship created unto good works that worketh in us to completion." There is an ending or terminus to the work that God has for US to do on the earth, yet there is no end to the relationship that we can have with God, even in the Afterlife. For we shall know, even as we are known. I'll record:

For unto us a child is born, unto us a son is given: and the government shall be upon his shoulder: and his name shall be called Wonderful, Counsellor, The mighty God, The everlasting

Father, The Prince of Peace.

Of the increase of his government and peace there shall be no end, upon the throne of David, and upon his kingdom, to order it, and to establish it with judgment and with justice from henceforth even for ever. The zeal of the LORD of hosts will perform this. Isaiah 9:6-7.

When it says of the increase of His government there shall be no end, I can't but help to think of certain American Presidents who have sought to spread democracy in the face of corrupt and shady foreign powers in the realm of global politics. A breath of fresh air from the sore history of colonialism and fascism from other countries. What will this government that shall reign from the seat of Jerusalem or the throne of David look like? According to scripture, how will the kingdom of God confront communism in China, or Socialism in North Korea. Not to mention the present theocracy and elective leadership in Iran.

Back to the scripture, these prophesies were written centuries before the birth and revealing of Christ. The display of His godhood and character on earth, as well as when He shall return. The government shall be upon his shoulders, spoke to how at his birth King Herod sought for His death, and at His death He met with Rome's ruling power in Jerusalem. He was a King born, and thrust into the earth, with His Kingdom yet afar off. But taught us to pray to the Father of lights, "thy Kingdom come, thy will be done, on Earth as it is in Heaven."

Some things to think about.

God Bless and Have a Great Day!

Chapter 42

Greetings everyone, Christ's impetus to tell others to worry not for the cares of life, or the necessities for the day such as food and clothing speaks to God's provision. We worry about how our mortgage or rent will be paid, our job security and relevance In the future, if retirement income will be enough to maintain and sustain our lifestyle. Christ has set Kingdom economic policy as the Kingdom and it's righteousness is first priority and order of business and after that is established , then all these things will be added.

I surmise, that He isn't saying not to plan or think about these things, but that when we put God's kingdom first it gives us perspective and peace and wisdom how to plan our lives. There are more important things to think about than food and clothing. We know and learn what is important and what we should focus on and how to better go about doing things to build our wealth and community because we know our purpose. We learn our role in the world and benefit from actively doing the work that He gives each of us to do. Even if it's simply to learn and observe at first.

Therefore I say unto you, Take no thought for your life, what ye shall eat, or what ye shall drink; nor yet for your body, what ye shall put on. Is not the life more than meat, and the body than raiment?

Wherefore, if God so clothe the grass of the field, which today is, and tomorrow is cast into the oven, shall he not much more clothe you, O ye of little faith?

Therefore take no thought, saying, What shall we eat? or, What shall we drink? or, Wherewithal shall we be clothed?

(For after all these things do the Gentiles seek:) for your heavenly Father knoweth that ye have need of all these things.

But seek ye first the kingdom of God, and his righteousness; and all these things shall be added unto you.

Take therefore no thought for the morrow: for the morrow shall take thought for the things of itself. Sufficient unto the day is the evil thereof. Mathew 6: 25; 30-34.

Yet Christ says, my yoke is easy and my burden is light. Does this mean there are no burdens or stress in ministry or life? No, if simply means we have less stress in living life and more power to carry out what we received from God to do. Certain ministry projects can be complex and very demanding, and even take weeks or months to plan. But if everyone is acting in their gifting or what they received form Heavens Kingdom, there will be certain lightness as everyone performs their administration of the Spirit, bang manifest for all. Same In secular society. People have talents, abilities, aptitudes and strengths and as conventional wisdom teaches, business leaders, and executives, should structure their organization and staff accordingly.

So among our many cares of the day, let us seek God's kingdom , and see how our perspective in life changes and how breakthrough and blessing began to overflow our life as we find the path God ultimately chose for US.

God Bless and Have a Great Day!

Chapter 43

Greetings everyone, --today's lesson deals more with the practicality of scripture, and God. Many times we in society get this idea that God is some far off, esoteric, illogical being who commands his subjects to do impossible and heart wrenching tasks to prove their devotion and loyalty. And in some cases, some may be able to make this argument, But in reality God through Christ is a down to earth, common sense, type of guy or God. He demonstrates his realness time and time again by interacting with common people with genuine kindness, by giving his disciples strait talk about His Father, the world, mankind and their folly, and finally by contradicting the self-righteous religious leaders of the day with examples from scripture that prove their ignorance and religious pride.

In today's example the Pharisees attempt to harass Christ over Him and His disciples picking corn on the Sabbath. Christ immediately instructs them with the lesson of David eating showbread from the temple, that thing which was unlawful for any but the priest to eat. In another place He talks about how the priest profanes the Sabbath and is found guiltless. With these instances; Christ ends the argu ment by saying, "the Sabbath was made for the Son of man, and not man for the Sabbath." I'll record:

At that time Jesus went on the sabbath day through the corn; and his disciples were an hungred, and began to pluck the ears of corn, and to eat.

But when the Pharisees saw it, they said unto him, Behold, thy disciples do that which is not lawful to do upon the sabbath day.

But he said unto them, Have ye not read what David did, when he was an hungred, and they that were with him;

How he entered into the house of God, and did eat the shewbread, which was not lawful for him to eat, neither for them which were with him, but only for the priests?

Or have ye not read in the law, how that on the sabbath days the priests in the temple profane the sabbath, and are blameless?

But I say unto you, That in this place is one greater than the temple.

But if ye had known what this meaneth, I will have mercy, and not sacrifice, ye would not have condemned the guiltless.

For the Son of man is Lord even of the Sabbath Day. Mathew 12:1-8

So, what we have here is a down to earth God that looks past all the bureaucracy and red tape of the law and religion and does what needs to be done to better aide mankind. What needs to be done, or what is needed, carrying not for policy, procedure, and protocols, although these things also have their place, because God is a God of order, yet he Createth the Chaos. Paradoxical I know, How can this concept help in our society? That instead of building more prisons, we increase funding to build and develop more day programs and build more Universities; who knows, maybe we increase mandatory criminal sentences to education, rehabilitation and mandatory therapy.

In terms of all the red tape and bureaucracy of healthcare, that we simply do what needs to be done to heal our patients if it be in our technological reach, that just like there be subsidized and unsubsidized loans for education, maybe there be low interest loans for major long-term care health related issues that terminate at the time of death with no further burden to the family. I'm spit balling here, but Who knows, maybe we stipend the poor with this Universal income idea, but make it mandatory that they be drug free and also that they be in some vocational, educational, or day program, charity service, or in some way bettering themselves and society in order to continue receiving funds.

These are just ideas for felons, the sick, and poor; what society looks upon as problems and the burden for tax payers. But what if we changed our thinking and forgetting all the rules of policy and red tape, and other legislature writings, to do what was needed even more so than we already do, that we help ourselves, help ourselves.

Christ's argument was that He was greater than the temple, greater than the law, and that He desires mercy and not sacrifices, ==not that we allow anarchy to grow rapidly, but that we tame with education and knowledge and seek the higher ideal. Of course prisons are a necessary evil for the hardened, unrepentant, unremorseful, extremely violent, and uncooperative, predatory offenders, but there is even hope for these, if after time, they are willing to change.

Some things to think about.

God Bless and Have a Great Day!

Chapter 44

Greetings Ladies and Gentlemen—Christ taught that His words were true and the living water of life. He taught that his words were bread and meat, in so many words, His words embodied Him incarnate God upon the Earth and His Spirit is known by the things He did and said. He taught in many formats; One being His preaching the beatitudes, and basic teachings in the Sermon on the Mount, and later in his ministry he taught by way of parables and dark sayings—mysteries about the Kingdom of God that always challenged his disciples to think deeply about their commitment as well as what great exploits could be done with God.

In today's lesson, we talk about the capstone teaching after all the Sermon on the Mt teachings. These teachings start with the beatitudes, and talk about showing off for God, forgiveness, meaning what you say, loving others, giving and praying in secret, storing your treasure in heaven, being anxious for nothing, not judging, putting God first, entering in at the straight gate, and discerning false prophets. These are the basic teachings given on the Sermon on the Mount when Christ first began his ministry that confronted the law and the prophets and summed up them up in two maxims; to love God with everything in you, and to love your neighbor as yourself.

Of course this seems like high flatulent fairy talk for the rebel, nevertheless, we want to point to how Christ said build your life upon these teachings to be considered wise, and the foolish builders who refuses such foundation will experience great fall during the day of trial and temptation. I'll record.

Therefore whosoever heareth these sayings of mine, and doeth them, I will liken him unto a wise man, which built his house upon a rock:

And the rain descended, and the floods came, and the winds blew, and beat upon that house; and it fell not: for it was founded upon a rock.

And every one that heareth these sayings of mine, and doeth them not, shall be likened unto a foolish man, which built his house upon the sand:

And the rain descended, and the floods came, and the winds blew, and beat upon that house; and it fell: and great was the fall of it. Mathew 7:24-27

So, just being real, sometimes the teachings of Christ can seem a bit overwhelming to the everyday person or unbeliever, or even the believer for that matter who is living a fun or "sinful" life, or who doesn't know anything about God or scripture. Although the bible teaches be ye not conformed to this world, but transformed by the renewing of your mind, it might be hard to prime the unbeliever or the ignorant cold turkey.   It takes divine influence, an impetus by God, a touch by God's Spirit.   With all this said, even the believer, myself included, struggle with issues; anger, forgiveness, lust, lascivisness, and faith.   But Christ challenges everyone to build their life on the rock of His words.   Reason being, when the storms hit; death, sickness, financial troubles, judgments, he says it his teachings that can and will sustain us.

Storms and mental illness can happen all on their own, but in the event of disaster the probability of nervous breakdown exponentially increases.   Christ says the foolish builder's house will fall because they built not their house on the rock.   It's been my experience , in my darkest hour, my house fell even though I knew, believed and followed Christ, but it was through grace, mercy and a lot of breaking of the religious and moral rules that I got back to a healthy state. This my not be everyone's story but strict adherence to the word of God in many ways I felt bound and limited my perspective although gave me insight. Who knows, maybe I was a bit naive.   But then again, maybe I had to mature in the word and world to develop and get a more keen understanding.   Moderation and tolerance are necessary for balance in life. Open mindedness to new ideals that seem to contradict or compromise our values, but ultimately confront and challenge character with reality.

Some things to think about.

God Bless and Have a Great Day!

Chapter 45

Greetings everyone,--today's lesson is more spiritual than others. Remembering when Christ said, "if you have not believed when I tell you earthly things, how shall you receive the heavenly things." Christ was referring to the mystery behind the rebirth experience to the curious Nicodemous who sought him in the middle of the night, In the passage of scripture covered in Ephesians, Paul talks about believers being dead in their sins and being caught up to sit together with Christ in heavenly places. What are the implications of this spiritual identity?

He further explains that this salvation is a gift from God, and that we are His workmanship. This speaks to the unconditional covenant of love that God makes and seals with the believer once we accept and believe in Him. We are his workmanship and the works that He created for us to do we are foreordained before the foundation of the world to walk in them. So, no man can boast, it is God that did it. I'll record:

Even when we were dead in sins, hath quickened us together with Christ, (by grace ye are saved ;)

And hath raised us up together, and made us sit together in heavenly places in Christ Jesus:

That in the ages to come he might shew the ex

ceeding riches of his grace in his kindness toward us through Christ Jesus.

For by grace are ye saved through faith; and that
not of yourselves: it is the gift of God:

Not of works, lest any man should boast.

For we are his workmanship, created in Christ
Jesus unto good works, which God hath before
ordained that we should walk in them. Ephesians 2:5-10.

So what does it really mean to sit in heavenly
places together with Christ? The word that is used
says that when we were dead in sin God quicken us up
together; or "suzoopoleo" which means, to reanimate
conjointly with. This implies that our spirits are res-
urrected with Christ and made to sit in heavenly places in God. This is not the after death experience, but
the here and now. What does it mean that our Spirits have access to the heavenliest? Does this affect
our dreams and proclivities? How our daily routines
transpire and our divine appointments? Also, does it
affect or interaction with other believers. I mean you
ever get that feeling that you know someone already
or they seem very familiar? Maybe it's because we sit
together or met each other in the Spirit in heavenly
places. The idea of telepathy comes to mind.

Some things to think about.

God Bless and Have a Great Day!

Chapter 46

Greetings Ladies and Gentlemen, today's lesson is a bit gritty as it deals with real life events of Ancient Day and can be related to by some in the sex industry today. We see God as a Unique and Creative being who has the ability to challenge His Servant to do the thing that is unorthodox, that doesn't make sense, or seems illogical, but ultimately speaks to a broader picture. The God of Israel, known to be Holy, High, and lifted Up, told the prophet Hosea to marry a women of whoredoms. He wanted His servant to marry a prostitute, someone with sex appeal, like an escort or an exotic dancer. God was having a little fun, and proving a point at the same time.

Well, maybe today, the average man with average moral standards would possibly sleep with a women given to extreme permiscuality, but to marry the prostitute takes courage, confidence, and extreme security within oneself, because more times than not , she will be unfaithful. And such was the case in the story of Hosea and the Gomer. She was given to seek out many lovers, and every time God told Hosea to go get his wife. He didn't say divorce her quietly, or shame her, or even beat her.—he said go get her. It was a picture of God's unconditional love for an adulterous Israel. And such were some of us as we ventured off from God and Christ and went our own way. I'll record:

The beginning of the word of the LORD by Hosea. And the LORD said to Hosea, Go, take unto thee a wife of whoredoms and children of whoredoms: for the land hath committed great whoredom, departing from the LORD.

So he went and took Gomer the daughter of Diblaim; which conceived, and bare him a son. Hosea 1:2-3

So, what would this story of the prophet and the prostitute look like in today's society and church age. A man with a higher standard of moral living marrying a women of immoral character in the area of marital fidelity. In one sense, oh what fun in the bedchambers? What man wouldn't love the passion of an experienced women, it's just the sharing of her that can become difficult. So the priest and the prostitute or the preacher and the escort getting married and having children.—It could work with God's love and forgiveness. Nevertheless, the time it would take to hammer out all the personality and lifestyle conflicts that might take some commitment and doggedness refusal to give up or let go. In most cases these women are broken and in need of guidance and love. Or, they are just about their money. LOL. I heard it said that God has a sense of humor and I believe He wants us to laugh and live. We have the choice of living cautiously or dangerously, circumspect or carless lives, to be cared for and evaluated by a loving God. Maybe it's not either or, but a little bit of it all. What and Whom shall we choose?

Some things to think about.

God Bless and Have a Great Day!

Chapter 47

Greetings everyone, today's lesson takes a look at the forgiveness of God and the infinite mercy we find with Him. Furthermore, we see that God takes His own advise in that as Christ tells Peter that he should forgive his brother seventy times seven (Mat. 18:22b), ultimately an infinite heart of forgiveness, God offers eternal love as well. In the proverb, "a just man falls seven times, and the Lord helps him out of all of them (Pro. 24:16a). What makes the just man just if he continues to be a moral failure? And what distinguishes him from the wicked? I think it is his desire to get up, it is his heart, and his drive for God. These things may seem like common sense; yet and still, God's mercy and love presents new opportunity to not be held down by guilt or brokenness but gives us strength to rise to the point of effectiveness. I'll record:

> For a just man falleth seven times, and riseth up again: but the wicked shall fall into mischief. Pro. 24:16.

Then came Peter to him, and said, Lord, how often shall my brother sin against me, and I forgive him? till seven times?

Jesus saith unto him, I say not unto thee, Until seven times: but, Until seventy times seven. Mat. 18:21-22.

So, what does it really look like; a just or a good man slipping up and falling down seven times and rising up again. All we have to do is take a look at our own lives. I think about business failure, companies going through bankruptcy, loss of job, inability to pay rent or mortgage, marital failure, and yet the just men shall rise. What about the moral failure and fall from grace of a true great leader whose at the center of attention such as a Pastor of a church or the civil servant cheating on their wife or embezzling funds, how do they rise from such disrepretable position? Well, it takes inner fortitude and tenacity not to give up in the face of conflict and defeat. With the help of God, nothing will be impossible, and maybe their rise exemplifies the mercy of God as well as encourages others what not to do. The Psalm says, I have said, Ye are gods, all of you are children of the Most High. But you shall die like men, and fall like one of the princes. (Psa. 82:6-7).

God Bless and Have a Great Day!

Chapter 48

Greetings everyone,=today's lesson deals with non-other than the supernatural and the paranormal. Not only does Christ a miracle worker, while he walked the dusty roads of Jerusalem and Judea, he also dealt with those spiritual powers that war against the soul of man. God is called the Father of Spirits (Heb. 12:9b) and we know there are spiritual manifestations of good and evil. Christ, the arm of God dealt very firmly with these demons and cast them out, told them to shut up, or had them bound, so they would not harm his lambs. It was his call, gifting, power and virtue that aided Him in these tasks. On one particular occasion, Christ healed a blind and dumb, man said to have a demon. And the man spoke and saw after the demon was cast out, but religious leaders said, it is by the prince of darkness that Christ has this power (Mat. 12:24). Christ began to teach a lesson, I'll record:

Then was brought unto him one possessed with a devil, blind, and dumb: and he healed him, insomuch that the blind and dumb both spake and saw.

And all the people were amazed, and said, Is not this the son of David?

But when the Pharisees heard it, they said, This fellow doth not cast out devils, but by Beelzebub the prince of the devils.

And Jesus knew their thoughts, and said unto them, Every kingdom divided against itself is brought to desolation; and every city or house divided against itself shall not stand:

And if Satan cast out Satan, he is divided against himself; how shall then his kingdom stand?

And if I by Beelzebub cast out devils, by whom do your children cast them out? therefore they shall be your judges.

But if I cast out devils by the Spirit of God, then the kingdom of God is come unto you.

Or else how can one enter into a strong man's house, and spoil his goods, except he first bind the strong man? and then he will spoil his house.

He that is not with me is against me; and he that gathereth not with me scattereth abroad. (Mat. 12:22-30).

So, Christ simply explains if Satan cast out Satan, how can his kingdom stand, a kingdom divided against itself would utterly fall. Immediately my mind leads me to think of our own national political struc ture. I know we have checks and balances for the reasons that too much power not corrupt one branch or office., whatever it may be; executive, judicial, or legislative. And our republic is such that it is divided into parties so that people can align with the party that most fits with their inner ideals.

And yet, sometimes, do we forget that we are on the same team. Impeachment of our leaders happen when rules are broken, and not to discredit policy; yet and still, I think that the executive office has certain privileged discretions that maybe the spirt of the law would allow, who knows. But every time we impeach our leader, does it not make us look weak and divided as a nation. Or the fact that the leader does whatever ill to get to that position. The world stand mocking our political exercise and legal push=ups, but we must remember we are the United States and not the Divided States of America.

Back to the lesson; Christ said that in order to take the house, the strong man must be bound. I think of military dictators, strong men that kept their people in fear and their corruption, embezzlement, murder, and genocides caused others and/or their own people to suffer; Hitler, Saddam, Milosevic, the Khomer Rouge, to name a few. Sometimes an individual, sometimes an organization like ISIS and Al Qaeda.

Christ being a king himself gave military strategy against the adversary and said the head or the strong man must be bound and then the house divided. This is why certain governments use methods of propaganda and sabotage to divide.

Ultimately, in the war of good and evil Christ said it by the Spirit of God that the devil is cast out. This is a better method than ancient doctors use to use of bloodletting and trepanation, to release the spirits from the blood and of the brain, body and humors as a method of healing. These techniques even caused the death of a U.S. president. As well as drilling holes in the skull to cure mental illness..

How far we have come in our technology yet, how things are the same in terms of problems we must deal with.

Some things to think about.

God Bless and Have a Great Day!

Chapter 49

Greetings everyone==today's lesson filled with more military strategy for life wisdom from Christ the King. In this passage of scripture he talks about counting the cost of discipleship. He uses the analogy of building a tower and in another example talks about a king making sure he has enough fortitude, resources, and back-up to meet twenty thousand, with ten thousand; unless he give terms of diplomacy.(my paraphrase). Well, I presume not to understand all these things about military science and global affairs, but when I first started to get serious about my Christian faith in college, years ago; I didn't foresee all that would happen to me. All I had was a little faith and courage, probably a little self-righteousness, and took up for the journey. I utterly fell, but God eventually helped me and and I'm still imperfect, but am reminded of the scripture in Isaiah;

Even the youths shall faint and be weary, and the young men shall utterly fall:

But they that wait upon the LORD shall renew their strength; they shall mount up with wings as eagles; they shall run, and not be weary; and they shall walk, and not faint. Isaiah 40:30-31

For which of you, intending to build a tower, sitteth not down first, and counteth the cost, whether he have sufficient to finish it?

Lest haply, after he hath laid the foundation, and is not able to finish it, all that behold it begin to mock him,

Saying, This man began to build, and was not

able to finish.

Or what king, going to make war against another king, sitteth not down first, and consulteth whether he be able with ten thousand to meet him that cometh against him with twenty thousand?

Or else, while the other is yet a great way off, he sendeth an ambassage, and desireth conditions of peace. Luke 14:28-32

God in Christ is truly a deadly God. He desires the willing sacrifice of death as a commitment. He desires one to take up their cross and follow him. It is not the physical death that I'm speaking of, but that of the self will, the handing over of the will in order to receive newness of life. This is easier said than done. It can be painful and it can hurt our feelings, our pride, our body sometimes, our finances, our fun. But thank fully it was not us hanging on the cross, being pierced in the side and spit upon and mocked. Christ just wants our life. A life for eternal life, our heart of faith, for His Eternal Fidelity.

In a modern world, where there are so many nuclear powers and we all be in the melting pot of global citizenship; so much so, that international laws may one day effect our daily lives, what are we to do to remain a Sovereign nation and not allow our country to be bought. Trillions of dollars in debt and what does it all mean for our children and our children's children.

Maybe we should send ambassadors of diplomacy instead of mercenaries of war. This does not mean we stand cowardly or fearful, but that we smart the problem and discover a solution rather than let our imperialistic addiction rage against our adversaries. That we love our foreign brother but set him straight in what we will and won't allow. Less someone lay there dead as Cain killed Able.

Alright, enough of my Soapbox,

God Bless and Have a Great Day!

Chapter 50

Greetings Ladies and Gentlemen,--today's lesson touches on the benefit of having a sparing buddy. This probably goes without saying, but one can only practice any sport or craft by themselves for so long, but when another comes along who has trained and been taught just as well as you, it challenges you to get better and exposes your weak and strong points. This can be done by a friendly or adversarial relationship, but the purpose of the match, whether it be verbal, or physical in some ways, such as; wrestling, tennis, fencing, boxing, chess or even gaming. The point is, the dual tests the strength of both partners and ultimately makes them both stronger. Likewise, the scripture in proverbs tells us that the countenance of a friend sharpens the face of another as iron sharpens iron. I'll record:

Iron sharpeneth iron: so a man sharpeneth the countenance of his friend (Pro. 27:17).

So Solomon once again gives us wisdom for the ages that can be considered common sense and things that were heard before. Essentially, two brains are better than one. You probably heard it said that certain executives and business men prefer to have smarter people around them so that they can be challenged in their product, acumen, and productivity. New ideas breed success and it is important to appreciate the critique as well as the compliment. Constructive criticism from a well-meaning friend goes a long way. And even the insult can be learned form, if thought about properly. Why do people say the things they say to us? Is it our character flaw they see, or their own insecurities? We were all created in the image of God and show forth His reflection, so staring at one another face to face is sort of looking in a mirror; though we be different, yet in many ways the same, male or female.

God Bless and Have a Great Day!

Chapter 51

Greetings Ladies and Gentlemen,-today we talk about the righteous indignation of Christ. Many times we look at anger as a problem; the proverb says, "anger rest in the bosom of a fool" (Ecc 7:9b). But, there is a time and place for everything, time for war, for peace, time to embrace and refrain from embracing" (Ecc 3:5b,8b). Injustice and oppression are things worthy to be angry at. The wrong and ill of society gives one the right to be angry, although this not necessarily be the wisest emotion to harbor in one's heart, nor is it the best way to smart the problem. Actually, anger can potentially further fuel the problem, but that we channel it into something good.

Christ became infuriated with the money changers robbing the people in the temple and overcharging for the animal sacrifices that were to be purchased. He became disruptive, turned the tables over, and yelled. He recked the place, in the sight of God, and many witnesses for and against Him. This episode gives us a precursor of what will happen to the evil on the earth when the glorified Christ returns to judge. I'll record:

And Jesus went into the temple of God, and cast out all them that sold and bought in the temple, and overthrew the tables of the moneychangers, and the seats of them that sold doves,

And said unto them, It is written, My house shall be called the house of prayer; but ye have made it a den of thieves (Mat. 21:12-13).

So, it can be said that Christ had a bit of a temper against things that were not right. But we know the scripture says he was without sin. It also says, "be angry and sin not" (Eph 4:26). What makes you angry anyway? Take a moment to think about it. What about that particular issue ticks you off? On the contrary, what doesn't make you upset, that you feel you should be boiling about? Anger in itself is not wrong; it's what we do with it. Just like money in of itself is not evil, the scripture says that, "the *love* of money, is the root of all evil (1Ti 6:10a). Essentially the placing it above God, and giving it preeminence in your heart.

In terms of seeing red, or blowing fuses, and getting hateful; all that is unnecessary and we need to exercise temperance and be able to control our emotions no matter what the cause or situation. Passion should not rule over us, but instruct and stimulate us possibly to act, our passions should be subject to our will and intellect. Even soldiers in time of war must not be ruled by emotion, because it would cloud their judgment, but we must focus our passions that we may execute the mission or task decisively and be more effective.

God Bless and have a Great Day!

Chapter 52

Greetings everyone—today we talk about the power of God and His ability to turn back the dial of life in healing. In the biblical example of Hezekiah the thirteenth king of Judah who ruled for 28 years; he had come to the end of his life and "God sent the prophet Isiah to tell him, "set your house in order, for you shall die and not live"(Isa 38:1). How gracious of God to the godly king that he allowed Hezekiah to prepare himself for death. Well, Hezekiah was not ready to enter the realm of Eternity and asked God to remember his heart that he followed His commands and God heard His prayer. The scripture below records what happen hereinafter, but what I do not include is how Hezekiah was known as a king who "trusted the Lord and cleave to the Him to never leave from following him" (2 Kings 18:5-6). This gave him a sort of Solomon status because the scripture says there was none to reign out of the kings of Judah like him. God ultimately gave Hezekiah 15 more years to live and as a sign allowed the shadow to go back on the dial of Ahaz ten degree. Not only did God heal Hezekiah but He took care of his enemy, Assyria (Ancient Iran). I'll record:

In those days was Hezekiah sick unto death. And the prophet Isaiah the son of Amoz came to him, and said unto him, Thus saith the LORD, Set thine house in order; for thou shalt die, and not live.

Then he turned his face to the wall, and prayed unto the LORD, saying,

I beseech thee, O LORD, remember now how I have walked before thee in truth and with a perfect heart, and have done that which is good in thy sight. And Hezekiah wept sore.

And it came to pass, afore Isaiah was gone out into the middle court, that the word of the LORD came to him, saying

Turn again, and tell Hezekiah the captain of my people, Thus saith the LORD, the God of David thy father, I have heard thy prayer, I have seen thy tears: behold, I will heal thee: on the third day thou shalt go up unto the house of the LORD.

And I will add unto thy days fifteen years; and I will deliver thee and this city out of the hand of the king of Assyria; and I will defend this city for mine own sake, and for my servant David's sake.

And Isaiah the prophet cried unto the LORD: and he brought the shadow ten degrees backward, by which it had gone down in the dial of Ahaz. , 2 Kings 20:1-6; 11.

So, have you ever had a near death experience where you met and cried out for God? There be a number of publications on the topic that explain in detail what certain individuals saw and felt during their time of death or unconsciousness. Some have had out of body experiences where they float around and can panoramically view the scene of the accident and the reaction of bystanders and loved ones. Others have met God's being and/or Christ himself in some form or fashion. Ironically, even reports from those who were not in particularly Christian or Religious, seem to also have had pleasant experiences of meeting welcoming passe3d dead family members and sort of had a life in review.

Hezekiah had an uncertain near death experience where God told him through the prophet Isiah his time was up. I can imagine that his life in review flashed before his eyes through he was not yet physically dead, he immediately cried out to God and God rewarded Hezekiah for "trusting" and "cleaving" to Him and extended his life. What if God had said no? What if Hezekiah didn't have the passed years of faithful and loyalty to God to fall back on like some of the kings of Judah who were wicked throughout their reign. Our years of service are a type of credit to God and seems to aide in His decision on the amount of blessedness or blessing in our life as well as our eternal reward in the life After.

This does not mean that everyone gets the healing, for suffering makes us perfect, however odd or unfair that may seem. Remember Christ suffered most.

If God warned us before our day of death, what would be our state of mind? How does one prepare for such an event and would you, as Hezekiah did, pray for more time?

`   Some things to consider, kind of eerie, I

God Bless and Have a Great Day!

Chapter 53

Greetings everyone,==it is known throughout Christ's ministry that he emphasized the importance of forgiveness, in order to be forgiven(Luk 6:37b). There are a few parables on the topic; one such parable Christ makes comparison of the Kingdom if God to a Lord coming to collect accounts from his servants. This servant could not pay even after selling all he owned, and begged for mercy and time from his Lord to pay. The gracious Master forgave the servant his debts, and that servant went off and abused his fellow servants who owed him and asked him for the same kindness.

Isn't this how some of us are some times? We receive the mercy of the court, but feel the next man that commits the same offence deserves their time. We get a break and look down upon others who barely make it and feel they don't work hard enough. We see someone in a similar situation as we have been and have the option to help ourselves, or fellow man or act as though we have not been there. Of course we cannot help everyone, but if everyone sort of found themselves in another and tried to help them out, whether it be a piece of advice, a monetary, nutritional, or some other tangible gift, or just a friendly conversation, you never know how far it could go or how it would change their life and society. I guess it is a remix of the "pay it forward" idea, only more personal, I'll record.

Therefore is the kingdom of heaven likened unto a certain king, which would take account of his servants.

And when he had begun to reckon, one was brought unto him, which owed him ten thousand talents.

But forasmuch as he had not to pay, his lord commanded him to be sold, and his wife, and children, and all that he had, and payment to be made.

The servant therefore fell down, and worshipped him, saying, Lord, have patience with me, and I will pay thee all.

Then the lord of that servant was moved with compassion, and loosed him, and forgave him the debt.

But the same servant went out, and found one of his fellow servants, which owed him an hundred pence: and he laid hands on him, and took him by the throat, saying, Pay me that thou owes.

And his fellow servant fell down at his feet, and besought him, saying, Have patience with me, and I will pay thee all.

And he would not: but went and cast him into prison, till he should pay the debt.

So when his fellow servants saw what was done, they were very sorry, and came and told unto their lord all that was done.

Then his lord, after that he had called him, said unto him, O thou wicked servant, I forgave thee all that debt, because thou desiredst me:

Shouldest not thou also have had compassion on thy fellow servant, even as I had pity on thee.

And his lord was wroth, and delivered him to the tormentors, till he should pay all that was due unto him.

So likewise shall my heavenly Father do also unto you, if ye from your hearts forgive not everyone his brother their trespasses. Mathew 18:23-35.

So, what are the consequences to being unforgiving, especially after we have received mercy? Well, besides being unforgiven by God, we break relationships, beat our own heart and soul by holding on to past resentment that can turn into hatred and eventually cause ones temper to be explosive or unmanageable. Who can stand before envy? (Pro 27:4b) Having people close to you that harbor secret resent and malice is a sure way to experience unexpected things being broken, sabotage, and just bad communication.

The best ways to get to the root of the problem is open dialogue, and if the problem persists, try to peacefully remove that person from your presence as soon as possible. That really is a drag when one party wants to be playful and the other party has anger and hatred and things get taken too far. But let us forgive, that we may be forgiven (Luk 6:37b).

God Bless and Have a Great Day!

Chapter 54

Greetings everyone, today we discuss the idea of small beginnings in terms of Christ's parable about the mustard seed. Christ put forth many parables; among them, a dark saying about the smallest of seeds, the mustard seed. Upon looking up images on the internet, the mustard seed is tiny in comparison to even an ordinary apple seed, but as Christ said, grows to the greatest of trees. Even a large tree with branches that allow the birds to nest in them. The point something small can transform into something great, because greatness was in it from the beginning; it just took time to develop. I'm not sure if this information is accurate, but the internet reports that it takes 8 years for the mustard seed to reach full development growing a few inches a day. 8 years may seem like a long time, butin reality and relative to the adult lifespan; it's not a long time at all. We are developing and growing our whole lives intellectually and in character and personality. I guess at some point in mid adulthood, maybe we reach a plateau in which we can always launch from. In the New Living Translation the prophetic book of Zechariah says, "despise not the day of small beginnings, the Lord desires to see the work begin" (Zec 4:10a).

So the point is, in life, like the old cliché saying goes, it's not how you start, but how you finish. What will we make of ourselves? How will we grow, even being the smallest of seeds; -how will we allow God to increase our hearts, and grow knowledge into us, and guide us with wisdom, and dig our roots with understanding that we may branch out in the end and at the climax of our lives other angels may rest in the beauty of our leaves, held by branches of strong support and a trunk that can withstand the winds and the rain. Christ, began to heal a man of blindness, and before he was completely healed he said, "I see men as trees walking" (Mar 8:24). I believe this man was given spiritual insight as he moved from the realm of darkness to sight in his receiving a miraculous healing from Christ, spitting on his eyes and touching them. I'll record the scripture in Mathew about the mustard seed.

Another parable put He forth unto them, saying, The kingdom of heaven is like to a grain of mustard seed, which a man took, and sowed in his field:

Which indeed is the least of all seeds: but when it is grown, it is the greatest among herbs, and becomes a tree, so that the birds of the air come and lodge in the branches thereof. Mat. 13:31-32

So, we understand that we need time to develop, but what happens when we cut our growth short, or stop progressing all together. When we stop learning and prospering in life we become like stagnant undis turbed water and ultimately; stale. There is a place for consistency and routine, and these are good things to have and keep, yet consistency and routine without growth or upward and/or forward momentum is an equivalent to being stuck in a rut. Newness and freshness comes from movement and experience, ideas, new things, outlooks and brave perspectives are what push and pull us forward.

God Bless and Have a Great Day!

Chapter 55

Greetings Folks, today we talk about unbelief and how it inhibits productivity, miracles, and hinders what God can or would do in the life of his people. Unbelief stops the party short. We see in the gospel of Mathew, Christ tells his disciples that in his home town, where people know him, he could not do many miracles because of their unbelief (Mat 13:58). Nazareth, where Christ was born and grew up; the community that knew his mother Mary, step-father Joseph, brothers and sisters; could not wrap their minds around the fact that little Jesus, the boy that used to go to temple, had made something of himself, and now all grown up in his own ministry, doing the bidding of the Father, with all miraculous power, wonder, and authority. Furthermore, he claimed to be the fulfillment of messianic prophesies, making himself equal with God, and declaring to be the Son of Man,-- God in the flesh.

They snuffed their noses, and said it couldn't be; maybe they said to themselves, he is no better than I am, what make's him so special? Why is he doing miracles, and prophesying about some Kingdom? Yet, is that not some of our jealous attitudes when someone in our circle or community experiences success. Of course not everyone has an envious heart, but not all our congratulators are genuinely happy for their fellow man. Instead of admiration, some harbor secret resent or hatred and it's sad, because that is the sin that overtook Cain to kill Able. I believe it is part of the sin or emotion behind Nazi and Islamic extremist hating Jewish people; is it jealousy and unbelief of God's words, that He said, "But thou Israel are my servant, Jacob have I chosen, the seed of Abraham my friend" (Isa 41:8). What drives such hatred and animosity? Ignorance, stupidity, history, what is it? The Ironic, or funny thing Is, well not so funny given the sore history; but interesting, is that some Belgian DNA studies suggest that Hitler had Jewish or even African Ancestry. These ideas come from Hitler's father being registered as an illegitimate child, thus Hitler's paternal grandfather remains unknown. Type in "Was Hitler Jewish?" on any browser's search engine and view what comes up.

Back to Nazareth, maybe it was the people's own insecurities that they did not believe the Christ. They didn't believe or know the prophesies that spoke of Him. My mind goes to the Old Testament prophetic scripture, that says, "My people perish for lack of knowledge" (Hos 4:6a). I'll record:

And when he was come into his own country, he taught them in their synagogue, insomuch that they were astonished, and said, whence hath this man this wisdom, and these mighty works?

Is not this the carpenter's son? Is not his mother called Mary? And his brethren, James, and Jo ses, and Simon, and Judas?

And his sisters, are they not all with us? Whence then hath this man all these things?

And they were offended in him. But Jesus said unto them, A prophet is not without honor, save in his own country, and in his own house.

And he did not many mighty works there because of their *unbelief*. Mat. 13:54-58

So, Christ could not because of the unbelief. This is a major principle, and I think often gets taken lightly. Unbelief and lack of faith is a major sin in God's eyes. Although forgivable, and God sheds more grace(unmerited gift or favor), it says that we don't know who God is, a God who can do the impossible. Our faith should be that we believe even if he chooses not to do the thing we ask of Him. The point is, no matter what we do, believe, say, or think; it does not change who God is, but it does effect what God may or may not do in our lives.

Some things to think about.

God Bless and Have a Great Day!

Chapter 56

Greetings everyone—In this episode, we learn some of God's character and even his thought process in revealing certain things to those who trust in Him and also what He allows depending ones relationship to Him. In short, God is a friendly, a gossip or water mouth and reveals secrets to trusted friends, and merciful for the sake of His own name and reputation. In the passage of scripture in Genesis, the three beings or theophonies have just left after telling Abraham and Sarah that they would have a son from their own loins, even despite their old age. As they begin to leave and head toward Sodom and Gomorra for judgment, The Word says, they talked among themselves (the three visitors) and God said, should I hide that thing which I do from Abraham. Right there, lets us know that God has things to tell us, and things about the immediate and even far hereafter that we can possibly know.

What is the condition and qualification for Abraham to receive this level of clearance to be privy to this information? God knew that Abraham was going to be great and that he would teach his children to follow after Him in righteousness (Gen 18:17-18). These two things that God knew about Abraham permitted him into the highest level of clerence known to man at that time. To know the demolition mission or seek and destroy af ter surveillance mission that these three visitors were about to go on. Abraham immediately began to plead for the city concerned about the civilians who were decent people, why should they all die God?, was Abraham's prayer. God heard Abraham and reasoned with him like a wise commander. Abraham stood in God's presence and negotiated for the lives of the innocent people until He got God to spare the city if 10 were found righteous. You can read in Genesis to get the back story on Sodom and Gomorra as well as to see what happened. But for this purpose, Abraham intercedes as High Priest and God reveals classified secrets. I'll record:

And the men rose up from thence, and looked toward Sodom: and Abraham went with them to bring them on the way. And the LORD said, Shall I hide from Abraham that thing which I do; Seeing that Abraham shall surely become a great and mighty nation, and all the nations of the earth shall be blessed in him? For I know him, that he will command his children and his household after him, and they shall keep the way of the LORD, to do justice and judgment; that the LORD may bring upon Abraham that which he hath spoken of him. And the LORD said, Because the cry of Sodom and Gomorrah is great, and because their sin is very grievous; I will go down now, and see whether they have done altogether according to the cry of it, which is come unto me; and if not, I will know. And the men turned their faces from thence, and went toward Sod om: but Abraham stood yet before the LORD. And Abraham drew near, and said, Wilt thou also destroy the righteous with the wicked? Peradventure there be fifty righteous within the city: wilt thou also destroy and not spare the place for the fifty righteous that are therein? And he said, Oh let not the Lord be angry, and I will speak yet but this once: Peradventure ten shall be found there. And he said, I will not destroy it for ten's sake. Genesis

And the LORD went his way, as soon as he had left communing with Abraham: and Abraham returned unto his place. 18: 16-24; 32-33.

So, how do we translate this happening into the likes of today? What is God itching to tell US? And what is the neccessary level of clearance to receive immediate prophesies about the future and what God is doing? Well, Holy men speak for God and to God. Men set apart that spend time in solitude, prayer, meditation and deep study, hear from God, as well as everyday people. Paul teaches in Corinthians that men should covet to prophesy (1Co 14:39), as we covered in another place. And fundamentally, aside from study of history, scripture, and currents; it takes a relationship with God and a gift of prophesy which is essentially the ability to hear from God and see through visions, dreams, and life, if He so allows or so reveals to you what He is saying. Sensitivity to the Holy Spirit. God still speaks to man and gives secret counsel, we are not all schizophrenic suffering from visual and auditory hallucinations; it's communication with the divine. I wonder how many of God's Old Testament prophet's if given a modern day psychiatric exam, Christ included, would be classified as psychotic, suicidal, schizophrenic, paranoid, grandiose, withdrawn, bipolar, multiple personality disorder, and even borderline. Who knows?

God's people can be peculiar, eccentric, and uniquely profound in their thinking and dealings. Not that they have a monopoly on originality, because some musicians, actors, business execs, and diverse professionals can be the same way. The point is, if people spend time with themselves and God long enough, working on some particular craft or doing next to nothing at all, there probably going to be, see, say, and think a little different than the everyday individual in society who simply dulls through the rat race of life.

Some things to chew on.

God Bless and Have a Great Day!

Chapter 57

Greetings everyone—today's lesson highlights the spiritual ability of Christ. We know and understand that although Christ was man he was also God in the flesh. There was no way he could accomplish such great things and do such exploits except that this be true. What does this mean for US? The fact that Christ, the lamb of God, lives in US, with all power and wisdom. Understand that it does not mean that we walk on water, or feed 5,000 with minimal resources; for these were works given for Christ to do; but maybe in another way, we do do these same miracles, and greater as Christ said in so many words, "You shall do this and greater, if you only believe" (Mat 21:21). Have you ever experienced a period of time in your life where it seems as though everything is going right, in finances, relationships are golden, few or no ministry problems, job and business opportunities are good and at an all-time high, and life is simply well,--perfect. This in my summation is the equivalent to walking on water. And while few have fed 5,000 with a few loaves and two small fish, there be many that preach and teach to hundreds and thousands today and feed people spiritual food that can sustain the soul with insight and develop the mind. I'll record:

But the ship was now in the midst of the sea, tossed with waves: for the wind was contrary.

And in the fourth watch of the night Jesus went unto them, walking on the sea.

And when the disciples saw him walking on the sea, they were troubled, saying, It is a spirit; and they cried out for fear.

But straightway Jesus spake unto them, saying, Be of good cheer; it is I; be not afraid. Mathew 14:24-27.

Have you ever experienced the phenomenal of figuratively walking on water. It must be a great feeling. To do what seem the impossible. As in this particular text Christ's disciples thought him to be a Spirit or Ghost walking toward them on the water, likewise, when one is figuratively walking on water in life, people wonder what spirit or power is behind them, for them, guiding, and/or influencing them. Christ said to his disciples when he reached them, "Be ye not afraid, it is I" (Mat 14:27).

I'm not talking about Celebrity Magic Shows, or sleight of hand, even though these be entertaining, but God is walking in US into divine appointments; there is evidence of His presence; Behold, it is He.

God Bless and Have a Great Day!

Chapter 58

Good morning folks,--today we talk about labor policy in God's eyes, jealousy, and God's goodness. The parable of selection for these topics is the house-holder who handed out tasks to work in his vineyard. Christ told this relating the householder to be the Lord, and the workers in the vineyard, those called to do God's work. Well, the story goes, that those who worked the longest, endured the brunt of the work, and sweated the most, presumed they would receive more payment than those who came later in the day, or who worked fewer hours, but let's see what God did I'll record:

> For the kingdom of heaven is like unto a man that is an householder, which went out early in the morning to hire labourers into his vineyard.
>
> And when he had agreed with the labourers for a penny a day, he sent them into his vineyard.
>
> And he went out about the third hour, and saw others standing idle in the marketplace,
>
> And said unto them; Go ye also into the vineyard, and whatsoever is right I will give you. And they went their way.
>
> And when they came that were hired about the eleventh hour, they received every man a penny.

But when the first came, they supposed that they should have received more; and they likewise received every man a penny.

And when they had received it, they murmured against the goodman of the house,

Saying, These last have wrought but one hour, and thou hast made them equal unto us, which have borne the burden and heat of the day.

But he answered one of them, and said, Friend, I do thee no wrong: didst not thou agree with me for a penny?

Take that thine is, and go thy way: I will give unto this last, even as unto thee.

Is it not lawful for me to do what I will with mine own? Is thine eye evil, because I am good?

So the last shall be first, and the first last: for many be called, but few chosen. Mat. 20:1-4; 9-16.

So, we have here a kind of economic policy that would not fly in America; as no senior level executive and entry level employee have the same salary. And it makes sense. And yet, there be some organizations who bring on professional, graduate and bachelor level talent and these employees or company assets will come in making more or equal pay because of their expertise and training. I've also spoke to veterans who've served in one branch or the other in the military; and their seems to be tension when you have younger officers in charge of enlisted who may trump their officers in age or education, but have not military or combat experience.

Who really knows the complexities, and details of these dynamics, but the spiritual point is, each individual should go to God for what they are to receive, and not worry or be jealous about their neighbor's or brother's salary. On the contrary, this is a tough statement to make in our modern world and economy, that is structurally stratified and where we often here about grievances for gender, race, and sexual orientation wage inequality and/or various forms of discrimination issues. Who knows, is it inequality, or is it the discretion of the business owner or "householder" to pay what they will with their own money per agreement, as suggested by Christ's parable? And yet, even still, If there is equal work being done, and all other things being equal; education, time on job, and performance, should there absolutely be equal pay? I'll let the business ethics committee decide. The idea is, as we discuss these biblical principles of God's kingdom policies, do they make sense when translated into our own economy, legislature, and society?

Some things to think about.

God Bless and Have a Great Day!

Chapter 59

Greetings Ladies and Gentlemen—today we talk about wisdom   from Solomon on issues of the heart. More specifically, what to do with the heart; and that is to "keep it." "Keep it" being opposite of the phrase, "he wears his heart upon his sleeve." Solomon warns that one should guard the secrets and issues of their heart because it keeps all of the "gongs on" of life. The will, thoughts, and plans are in a man's heart. The secrets of a man's soul, his love and hate, passions, and fears or lack thereof flow from his heart. The fleshly treasure chest of ethereal things should not be left wide open or easily broken into.

Of course there is a time that a man has a heart to heart with women, or with a man, as iron sharpens iron. We keep our strength when we keep our heart. Unless we pour it out to heal others and receive strength back again from God and other's pouring into us. I'll record:

Keep thy heart with all diligence; for out of it are the issues of life. Pro. 4:23

\

So, we are informed to keep our heart. The Hebrew word to keep is "natsar" which carries the meaning to guard, protect, maintain, hidden thy keep. Alright, so what about therapy? In some cases we see the heart is broken , wounded, and in need of healing. Another scripture say "The heart is deceitful above all things, and desperately wicked: who can know it?"(Jer 17:9). The point is, sometimes a doctor is needed spiritual or psychiatric to help perform surgery and take apart a piece of the heart and delve into the life and mind of the broken to put it back together. The Spirit of God can work with those experienced in this type of operation.

Relationships break the heart, disappointments, feeling unfulfilled, insecurities, and fatigue through weariness weighs it down; but laughter and good food with a little wine is good for the soul, along with a nice wallet also according to Solomon (Ecc. 10:19). Eternal joy comes from one's soul and spirit being enjoined with Christ, accepting Him in the heart brings peace and a relationship with God. Not only does Solomon say keep the heart, but he says with all diligence. This implies to me that there should be an investigative gathering of understanding and intellectual resources to aide in the issues of life, jewels to be kept for a later time. Diligently gathered for this fleshly treasure chest, called the heart.

God Bless and Have a Great Day!

Chapter 60

Greetings everyone—today we speak on the topic of God's omniscience and how He and His Angel are always watching us on our daily movements; comings and goings. The Psalm says, "though knowest my thoughts afar off" (Psa 139:2). Knowing this and dealing with the reality that man's thoughts can be impure, and man cannot always control his what he thinks, it becomes an issue or question of integrity. Integrity; what we do when we think no one is watching or will find out, but we know that God is always watching US. And Moreover, the scripture says, "He pondereth our goings"(Pro 5:21).

Think about it, the Creator of the Universe, sits around thinking about where we are going and what we are doing for the day. He delights in US. The word pondereth used in the Hebrew is "palac" and it means, to weigh out; to compare accurately. The image is that of scales or a balance being weighed. On the balance of justice the seventh zodiac sign in astrology paints a clear picture. Interesting that God would put our heart upon a scale and determine it's weight with the sacrifice of Christ. What is our heart, that would balance with Christ; although our heart in no way compares to Christ, if Christ is in our heart then the scales balance with the weight of His sacrifice. I only presume these things and it's my interpretation from the book; who knows how "God weighs the Spirits" (Pro 16:2) in His divine courts and scales of His own Justice and Righteousness. I'll record:

For the ways of man are before the eyes of the

LORD, and he pondereth all his goings. Pro. 5:31

Every way of a man is right in his own eyes: but the LORD pondereth the hearts. Pro. 21:2

If thou sayest, Behold, we knew it not; doth not he that pondereth the heart consider it? And he that keepeth thy soul, doth not he know it? and shall not he render to every man according to his works? Pro. 24:12

So, in these texts we see God as a psychoanalytical judge of the heart who considers the thoughts of mankind. His Omniscience and Omnipresence leaves us naked before His presences even when fully clothed, because He sees through US and gets to the core of the soul. He watches to guard US and know our nature whether it is good or evil; only he knows the true thoughts and intents of the heart (Heb 4:12b). Sometimes even man himself knows not what manner of spirit he has, as when the sons of Zebedee wanted to reign down fire from heaven as Elijah did, to consume those that did not receive Christ. And Christ said,

> "You know not what manner of Spirit ye are of, for the son of man came not to destroy life but to save them (Luke 9:55-56).

So, how can we know what manner of spirit we are;-- but by our relationship with God, and the study of His words? Who knows, maybe we see ourselves in the bible just like people can relate or see themselves in certain literary creations, movies, and TV shows.

Back to the idea of integrity, we know that God rewards us openly what we do in secret, good or bad, for all the secrets of our heart are manifest before Him. So, we might as well be ourselves and look toward and depend upon His mercy, because, "no one is good, but one, that is God" (Mar 10:18).

God Bless and Have a Great Day!

Chapter 61

Greetings everyone,--today we talk a little bit about doctrine with respect to the divine gifts of grace and faith. The text comes from Romans and essentially says that by faith are we saved and not by works, This sounds like Martin Luther, the old Germen professor, theologian, and priest. The scripture points to Abraham as one who believed and was rewarded with righteousness, it further says, in so many words, if one works for salvation it is as a debt that can never be paid off. And finally that God justifies the ungodly who believe. His faith is his ticket for righteousness, essentially because he trust in God to do what He has promised to do through Christ. This revelation in my eyes sort of loosens up the idea of strict adherence to the Word. I mean, don't get me wrong, I know that Christ says, "narrow is the way that leadeth to life, and few there be that find it..."(Mat 7:14). The point is, God forgives those who believe, and Faith in Christ is so powerful that it overshadows our sin. I'll record:

For what saith the scripture? Abraham believed God, and it was counted unto him for righteousness.

Now to him that worketh is the reward not reckoned of grace, but of debt.

But to him that worketh not, but believeth on him that justifieth the ungodly, his faith is counted for righteousness. Rom. 4:3-5

So, what does it really mean that God covers the ungodly who believes; Does it mean that we live whichever way we choose to live and just count on our faith to handle our inward and outward inappropriateness? Is this passage of scripture giving a free pass to an ungodly lifestyle, or does It just cover the inception of our walk with God? We know that God's arm of salvation lifts us up when we fall, but our mind and soul cannot have a continual intent on misusing the grace and mercy of God. Although Christ says, "there be none good, but God"(Mat 19:17), he does expect us to love Him and our neighbor. With these two laws on our minds, it's plausible that our life can get better over time. By loving God and showing kindness to others, because of the love of God in our hearts.

Some things to think about.

God Bless and Have a Great Day!

Chapter 62

Greetings everyone,--today we look at Peter's theme on the steps to godhood; spiritual and character development, knowledge of God and self-control, the ability to wait, love, the ability to give; and ultimately the product of godliness. Of course I have paraphrased the steps of progression in which Peter has recorded in his second letter, but we can get the point. One must tame their soul unto a diligent quest and thirst for knowledge and development and then display these new found truths in our living by being kind to the world around us, our fellowman, and then attempt to imitate God, less we be mean and prideful gods; He said "I have said, Ye are gods, all ye are children of the Most High"(Psa. 82:6). What would "God or Christ do?" as the old saying goes, but it can help us, if we know Him; direct our divine nature as we have an entrance provided for us into the Kingdom of God and ministry.

Of course we normally take godhood to mean, Universal Authority, unnatural beauty and strength, power, immortality, and perfection and luck in our craft or doings. Though we all be children of the Most High, there is only one God who now reigns in the heavens and but there be kings, priests, and prophets in position upon the earth who shall also reign with Him in the Millennium or be set down depending on their faith or lack thereof in Christ; It all starts with faith, Peter says, add to your faith, virtue. I'll record.

Whereby are given unto us exceeding great and precious promises: that by these ye might be partakers of the divine nature, having escaped the corruption that is in the world through lust.

And beside this, giving all diligence, add to your faith virtue; and to virtue knowledge;

And to knowledge temperance; and to temperance patience; and to patience godliness;

And to godliness brotherly kindness; and to brotherly kindness charity.

For if these things be in you, and abound, they make you that ye shall neither be barren nor unfruitful in the knowledge of our Lord Jesus Christ. 2 Pet. 1:4-8.

So, what does godhood look like today? Who are the angels among US. Divine leaders, business leaders, statesmen, the graduates, Athletes and Artists, are the great in society and even the common sons and daughters of God. Even though God say in the psalms, "ye all are children of the Most High" (Psalm 82:6), do we claim our godhood, or shall we humbly walk the earth as man without knowledge of the di

vine and the authority he put in each of us who believe. Ignorant of His new life, and the life to come.
What is your nature and evolution that you belong to
the kindness of the Most High? What fruit has your
tree produced and is it good or evil that you practice?
I presume not to call myself anything but a son of
God in Christ and a joint-heir to the throne because
of what scripture says, and yet it says and names US
so much more as inheritors of His divine riches and
grace. I know my morality and spiritual ability fall
short of His glory: upon his grace, I depend; His faith
is a gift from above.

God Bless and Have a Good Day!

Chapter 63

Greetings everyone; today we discuss what it means to discover new information about God, the world, and how this can affect our lives. On the surface, may seem boring, I know, but stay tuned, it is an unearthing story. How will we let a new epiphany, vision, or word change our mind set. When new knowledge is found, that infuses our perspective and even our emotional response to things, how do we allow this to implement transformation in our lives? Whether incremental or suddenly, how does it apparently condition us for something different in life? Such was the case in the story of Josiah, the king which was set upon the throne of Judah at 8 years old and reigned for 31 years. He was a king who did good like his fore-father David in the sight of the Lord, unlike kings before him who did evil, like Ahaz, Ammon, and Manasseh.

So, as the case goes, work gets done on the temple by Josiah's staff and the book of the law is found, When Joseph comes into this knowledge of God and saw how past kings had hid the word of God, and how Judah had slipped so far from practice of the Truth, he ripped his clothes and cried out. He immediately told his staff to seek God concerning this matter. I'll record:

Josiah was eight years old when he began to reign, and he reigned thirty and one years in Jerusalem. And his mother's name was Jedidah, the daughter of Adaiah of Boscath.

And he did that which was right in the sight of the LORD, and walked in all the way of David his father, and turned not aside to the right hand or to the left.

And Hilkiah the high priest said unto Shaphan the scribe, I have found the book of the law in the house of the LORD. And Hilkiah gave the book to Shaphan, and he read it.

And Shaphan the scribe shewed the king, saying, Hilkiah the priest hath delivered me a book. And Shaphan read it before the king.

And it came to pass, when the king had heard the words of the book of the law, that he rent his clothes.

Go ye, enquire of the LORD for me, and for the people, and for all Judah, concerning the words of this book that is found: for great is the wrath of the LORD that is kindled against us, because our fathers have not hearkened unto the words of this book, to do according unto all that which is written concerning us. 2 Kings 22:1-2; 8; 10-11; 13.

So, what is our response to the epiphany or new knowledge we didn't know? How would it affect you, if you thought the world was one way, and found it was completely different? What if this was the case with God or Society? It's kind of like a California turnaround in a good movie; instances can be found in; *The Sixth Sense* **and** *Fight Club***. It totally blows your mind and causes you to re-adjust your perception, even your behavior. You want to continue as things were, but the current paradigm is different and old behaviors or ideas don't work like they used to. It can be frustrating and liberating at the same time, but there is the time that it takes to acclimate to a new set of rules. Imagine that people who join the military, or travel to a new country or even domestically to a new city or town may experience this same type of phenomenon on some level; experiencing a new culture, with language, food, dress, religion and key subtleties that have to be picked up on before comfortability between you and the people can be reached.**

And yet, I got a little off topic, Josiah found the law and saw how drastically off his society was and made changes. What happens to your life when you look into the mirror of the Word, then look up at society, and then into your heart and life.

Some things to think about.

God Bless and Have a Great Day!

Chapter 64

Greetings everyone,--today's we take a peak at the life of Jehoshaphat, a king of Judah who was considered good for some of the deeds and policies he implemented. We see from the biblical example that good or godly kings and governments want their people educated or instructed in the ways of God. Jehoshaphat is known for setting up and organizing judges and priest, those from the house of Levi; Levites all throughout the southern kingdom to judge the proposal and teach the law which was I presume the Pentateuch, first five books of the old testament, said to be written by Moses. An enlightened people means an enlighten nation; for the scripture says, "my people are destroyed for a lack of knowledge"(Hos 4:6a).

At one time the bible was taught in the public school system. In the seventeenth century, the founding fathers thought that the bible displayed patterns for the destinies of mankind. During the 1700-1900, the bible was taught in private schools, church schools, and our public school s used as a textbook. What would we be as a people if more people had knowledge of God and knew or even had an elementary understanding of the scriptures. What a greater nation and people we would be if we would not be so judgmental, self-righteous, and hateful; and have a true understanding of the power and love, grace and mercy of God.

I think we would be better off. Maybe there would be less crime, less drugs storming our communities, or who knows, maybe the youths would rebel. Even still, knowledge of God and spiritual things couldn't hurt. Like the scripture says, "train a child in the way they should go, and when they are old, they will not depart from it" (Pro 22:6). I'll record in Chronicles, the words of Jehoshaphat:

Nevertheless there are good things found in thee, in that thou hast taken away the groves out of the land, and hast prepared thine heart to seek God.

And Jehoshaphat dwelt at Jerusalem: and he went out again through the people from Beersheba to mount Ephraim, and brought them back unto the LORD God of their fathers.

And he set judges in the land throughout all the fenced cities of Judah, city by city,

And said to the judges, Take heed what ye do: for ye judge not for man, but for the LORD, who is with you in the judgment.

Wherefore now let the fear of the LORD be upon you; take heed and do it: for there is no iniquity with the LORD our God, nor respect of persons, nor taking of gifts.

Moreover in Jerusalem did Jehoshaphat set of

the Levites, and of the priests, and of the chief of the fathers of Israel, for the judgment of the LORD, and for controversies, when they returned to Jerusalem.

And he charged them, saying, Thus shall ye do in the fear of the LORD, faithfully, and with a perfect heart.

And what cause whosoever shall come to you of your brethren that dwell in their cities, between blood and blood, between law and commandment, statutes and judgments, ye shall even warn them that they trespass not against the LORD, and so wrath come upon you, and upon your brethren: this do, and ye shall not trespass.

And, behold, Amariah the chief priest is over you in all matters of the LORD; and Zebadiah the son of Ishmael, the ruler of the house of Judah, for all the king's matters: also the Levites shall be officers before you. Deal courageously, and the LORD shall be with the good. II Chron. 19:3-11.

So, we see Jehosaphat was a king that administrated God's servants into the culture by giving the lectern positions throughout the country and positions of municipalities. How could this legally translate into today's modern society. Instead of Christian studies, perhaps we need to make it religious studies and tech the bible,

Islam, Buddhism, Taoism, and Hinduism, so that our children would be a type of global citizen, with awareness and not narrow minded or ignorant and hateful. We know many people fear what they do not know, who knows what it could do for society and the love that might be shed abound. Plus, with the rising Muslim tension arising in Iran and the past wars in Iraq, Afghanistan, Kuwait, and the Middle East in general, it's probably wise to give our children some background, so that we can be an informed and intelligent people.

These ideas may advance and develop us further as a nation, it's not that we don't already do them, but maybe we just offer this education sooner. This type of evolution might even enhance our economy because of the brotherhood that can exist amongst mankind and other nations, increased global trade because of understanding of culture. Maybe this religious study idea becomes a global mandate to help other nations understand the culture of other peoples and build bridges and treaties of peace instead of missiles and silos of war. Obviously, I'm not suggesting that we disarm ourselves, leaving us helpless to defend ourselves with strength and aggression, but simply that we attempt to instruct and place the tool of knowledge within the hands of our youth and even all over the world, to bring up, if at all possible, a hateless or less hateful generation. Who knows?

Of course these are always contrary options; to remain ignorant of our neighbors, dumb down our citi zenry, and live on being ignorant of the world around us seems a little backward in today's modern and technologically advanced age. I get that we should mind our own business, like any good neighbor should not meddle in the affairs of another, but when we are the 600 pound gorilla in the room, shouldn't we know who else is in there? Doesn't even military strategy suggest that we know the adversary and even befriend him if we can with diplomacy. But of course, this is an old idea, and something that we already practice, or do we? Who knows?

Some things to think about.

God Bless and have a Great Day!

Chapter 65

Greetings everyone; today we talk about God's conditional blessing that Israel received upon crossing the Jordan and making it into their land of promise and blessing, milk and honey, or (oil and money:-),--Canaan. Of course this is an Old Testament scripture that was conditioned and dependent upon Israel's obedience to God's commands and their continued acknowledgement of God, remembering to never forget what God had done for them. They had spent 40 years in the wilderness, failed in the first attempt to go into the land, their children made to watch their parents who had not believed, and complained against God eventually die off. And now it was their turn to believe and follow God.

And haven't we all reached that point in our lives where we have been through some things, failed a few times, but finally we feel that God is doing something new and permanent, and all he is saying is, "don't forget what I did for you, remember me, acknowledge me, and I will continue to help and bless you." He has given us power to gain wealth (Deu 8:18). Some have realized this truth; some of us are trying to attain it, practice it, and live it out to the full. Some of us, do not realize the wealth that we already possess, even though it may not yet be in riches of the massive influx of capital gains, but in family, health, shelter, safety, intelligence, access to opportunity, and a plethora of other things we take for granted on a daily basis by just breathing and being alive in a free nation. I'll record:

All the commandments which I command thee this day shall ye observe to do, that ye may live, and multiply, and go in and possess the land which the LORD aware unto your fathers.

And thou shalt remember all the way which the LORD thy God led thee these forty years in the wilderness, to humble thee, and to prove thee, to know what was in thine heart, whether thou wouldest keep his commandments, or no.

Therefore thou shalt keep the commandments of the LORD thy God, to walk in his ways, and to fear him.

For the LORD thy God bringeth thee into a good land, a land of brooks of water, of fountains and depths that spring out of valleys and hills;

A land of wheat, and barley, and vines, and fig trees, and pomegranates; a land of oil olive, and honey;

A land wherein thou shalt eat bread without scarceness, thou shalt not lack any thing in it; a land whose stones are iron, and out of whose hills thou mayest dig brass.

When thou hast eaten and art full, then thou shalt bless the LORD thy God for the good land which he hath given thee.

Beware that thou forget not the LORD thy God, in not keeping his commandments, and his judgments, and his statutes, which I command thee this day:

Lest when thou hast eaten and art full, and hast built goodly houses, and dwelt therein;

And when thy herds and thy flocks multiply, and thy silver and thy gold is multiplied, and all that thou hast is multiplied;

Then thine heart be lifted up, and thou forget the LORD thy God, which brought thee forth out of the land of Egypt, from the house of bondage;

And thou say in thine heart, My power and the might of mine hand hath gotten me this wealth. (Duet. 8:1-2; 6-14;17).

And the truth is ladies and gentlemen, I am still imperfect and in need God's grace and mercy and also am in need and strongly desire his rich blessing upon my life; I try to daily acknowledge Him. I claim not perfection. Salvation is not conditional once it is received, but a gift of grace; not that I believe this because it fits my morality or lifestyle, but that If God allows one to come to Him and put His spirit inside of that person, it was by God's eternal foreknowledge that brings that person into their destiny.

God meets us in our sin, spiritually dead life, or awakened life, and gives us the gift of faith, and then slowly transforms our thoughts, our heart, and our life for Him. God's blessings are also a gift and an act of kindness that he gives us for our joy and His guidance, and distinguishes us as his children in the World. When we ask for God's blessing we are asking for God's will and for Heaven to be in the Earth. So God considers us His seed and offspring.

Some things to think about.

God Bless and have a Great Day!

Chapter 66

Greetings everyone,-- today we discuss how God calls things that are not, as though they were(Isa 46:10). It's not quite a duplicate to our Daniel study, but along the same lines. God deals in future events with his prophet by revealing things to them in visions, dreams, auditory and visual hallucinations and then speaks through them to tell the future. Such was the case in Isaiah's life as he prophesied many things including the birth, life, crucifixion, glorious future rule of Christ, and in addition, among many other things, the rebuilding of the temple in Jerusalem under decree by Cyrus.

Cyrus was not yet born, in fact 150 years before he was conceived the prophesy was made. There was policy under his leadership for the Jews to return from captivity from Babylon to go back and rebuild, with his financial and moral support as accounted for in Ezra. Wikipedia calls him a military and political genius and he didn't even know the God of Israel, but God in His sovereignty, still used Him for His and Jacob's name sake. As the scripture says in Daniel,"God rules in the kingdom of men" (Dan 4:17). What is God doing in the Heavens and in the Kingdom of men in this hour of history? Weather we consider Iran(Ancient Persia), who seeks to develop nuclear weapons and make decisions to either stand down or respond to US striking down one of their key generals, Qassem Soleimani, who was responsible for the training of militias and oversaw proxies of Iranian foreign militia groups in Iraq and abroad in the Middle-East, and was on the way to harm Americans. Or we consider North Korea threatening to launch a new secret weapon and under the leadership of Kim Jong Un seeks to weasel out of their denuclearization deal.

What will be the ultimate arrangement of nations in the middle east, far east, Europe, Latin America, and the west in this new age and will there be peace that cover the land? Only God knows, and can cure our anxieties for war, and keep our nation in safety and in a position of strength; a model for political, economic, and military fitness for the world. I'll record:

Thus saith the LORD, thy redeemer, and he that formed thee from the womb, I am the LORD that maketh all things; that stretcheth forth the heavens alone; that spreadeth abroad the earth by myself;

That frustrateth the tokens of the liars, and maketh diviners mad; that turneth wise men backward, and maketh their knowledge foolish;

That confirmeth the word of his servant, and performeth the counsel of his messengers; that saith to Jerusalem, Thou shalt be inhabited; and to the cities of Judah, Ye shall be built, and I will raise up the decayed places thereof:

That saith to the deep, Be dry, and I will dry up rivers:. That saith of Cyrus, He is my shep herd, and shall perform all my pleasure: even saying to Jerusalem, Thou shalt be built; and to the temple, Thy foundation shall be laid.

Thus saith the LORD to his anointed, to Cyrus, whose right hand I have holden, to subdue nations before him; and I will loose the loins of kings, to open before him the two leaved gates; and the gates shall not be shut;

I will go before thee, and make the crooked places straight: I will break in pieces the gates of brass, and cut in sunder the bars of iron:

And I will give thee the treasures of darkness, and hidden riches of secret places, that thou mayest know that I, the LORD, which call thee by thy name, am the God of Israel.

For Jacob my servant's sake, and Israel mine elect, I have even called thee by thy name: I have surnamed thee, though thou hast not known me.

I am the LORD, and there is none else, there is no God beside me: I girded thee, though thou hast not known me: Isiah 44:24-28; 45: 1-5.

Truly God is a God who "maketh the sun to rise

on the evil and good, and sendeth it to reign on the just and the unjust" (Mat 5:45). Cyrus, leader or Persia (Ancient Iran) was gifted with, "treasures of darkness and hidden riches of secret places" (Isiah 35:3a). I wonder what these hidden treasures and riches were. Were they the spoils from Media=Persia taking Babylon and that were in the Nebuchadnezzar and Darrius's kingdom; who knows? The point is, quite simply, God knows the future, so we should know God, and maybe he will reveal unto US, what he is doing, or will do in the earth. The scripture says, "Ask me of things to come concerning my sons, and concerning the work of my hands, command ye me"(Isa. 45:11).

Just some thoughts, but what are the implications of a modern day Cyrus arising from Iran and being Pro-Israel, and helping to solve the Palestenian-Isreali land conflicts; Investing oil and resources to unite as sons of Abraham. Iraq and all of the middle east, what if the original sons of Abraham could stop all their infighting and have a sort of family reunion and shock the world with a united stand for God and for Peace. I know it's cliché, "Peace in the Middle East, but What if, who knows? What would happen if there were sudden and massive Islamic and Jewish conversion to Christianity, or What if something unorthodox happen that were to prolong the tides of even biblical prophecy and these Middle-Eastern nations who derived from the sons of Abraham;-- namely Isaac, Ishmael, Jacob and Esau were to band to gather in brotherly love; for they are of the same bloodline, though the Messiah, was prophesied to come through the seed of Isaac(Gen 17:19). And yet, Princes were to come through Ishmael as well (Gen 17:20).

What if it started with American diplomacy, and through education and philanthropy, we democratized the world, and every land and nation was safe to live, visit, and trade. Of course these are far out ideas, given the in-trenched history, massive blood-shed, and current mindset, culture, corruption, and political arrangement of some foreign governments; particularly in the Middle-East, but who knows, with God, nothing will be impossible (Luk. 1:37). He said there would be a day that "nation shall not lift up sword against nation, and they shall not learn war any more."(Isa 2:4) Unfortunately, in light of current circumstances, that day is not today, January of 2020.

And yet, man in his nature finds it hard to give up the study of war. It's exhilarating and exciting to know the methods of strategic offence and defensive measures, progress, and accomplishment of the mission's targets through operational and tactical intelligence, though it bring upon casualty and death. And maybe it's just that, we make war intellectual and make training the practice of game theory, and war theatres for those thirsty for such rush and adrenaline; but that there be no brutal slaughtering of innocent lives, or our soldiers, unless absolutely necessary, not that we would ever be slaughtered, but that we would not be carelessly sent without being fully prepared and equipped to meet the enemy. Or is war the necessary evil, as Christ said, there will be "wars and ru mors of wars, be not troubled the end is not yet" (Mat 24:6) What generation will decide different? Though he did not say what type or kind of wars. Is it that we benefit economically from war, and it cuts down on overpopulation, or is it all about the money and the oil? Or is it solely about defending ourselves and our allies against enemy combatants who would want to do us harm. Who knows?

What shall we do with this sort of potential power and who wants to know, who can tell, and set in order these things that shall be as God's ancient prophets did back in Ancient of Day. He has said, "Those that know God shall do exploits in the earth" (Dan11:32).

God Bless and Have a Great Day!

-The End-

Note from the Author:

Dear Reader,

Thank you for journeying with me through this series. Assuming you've read Vol. I. I have tried to communicate what I believe God has given me to say. Having a ministerial background, I know at times my pros can sound preachy, but I really do try make it feel like a down to earth conversation, a sharing of ideas if you will.

Well, off to the next book, I hope you will stick with me, as I have many book ideas and will jump between biblical and secular topics as you can see in this except hereafter; The Writings of Antonio Vol. III *(US Presidents, their Generals, and their Wars)***. I hope you enjoy and purchase the next book. Happy Reading!**

The Writings of Antonio Vol. III

US Presidents, Their Generals,

and

Their Wars

Dedicated To:

Society in General

and

The Curious and Thirsty for Historic Knowledge

To the Historian, Scholar, and Student

To the Prophet and the Priest

And Every Statesman

And to my Kids:

Imani, Nathan, Ophelia, and Sonia

Contents

a.   **Daniel Brent- 1825**

b.   **Henry Clay – 1825-1829**

7.   **Andrew Jackson – 1829-1837**

     a.   **James A. Hamilton – 1829**

     b.   **Martin Van Buren –1829-1831**

     c.   **Edward Livingston – 1831-1833**

     d.   **Louis McLane – 1833-1834**

     e.   **John Forsyth - 1834-1837**

8.   **Martin Van Buren 1837-1841**

     a.   **John Forsyth - 1837-1841**

9.   **William Henry Harrison - 1841**

     a.   **Jacob L. Martin - 1841**

     b.   **Daniel Webster – 1841**

10.   **John Tyler**

     a. **Daniel Webster – 1841-1843**

     b. **Hugh S. Legare – 1843**

     c. **William S. Derrick – 1843**

     d. **Abel P. Upshur – 1843-1844**

e. John Nelson – 1844

f. John Calhoun – 1844 – 1845

11. James K. Polk – 1845-1845

    a. James Buchanan – 1845 – 1849

12. Zachary Taylor – 1849 - 1850

    a. John M. Clayton - 1850

13. Millard Fillmore – 1850-1859

    a.   John M. Clayton – 1850

    b. Daniel Webster – 1850-1852

    c. Charles M. Conrad – 1852

    d. Edward Everett – 1852 – 1853

14. Franklin Pierce – 1853 - 1857

    a. William Hunter - 1853

    b. William L. Marcy - 1853 - 1857

15. James Buchanan - 1857 - 1861

    a. Lewis Cass - 1857 - 1860

    b. William Hunter - 1860

c. Jeremiah S. Black – 1860 – 1861

16. Abraham Lincoln – 1861 -1865

   a. William H. Seward – 1861 -1865

17. Andrew Johnson – 1865 – 1869

   a. William H. Seward – 1865 – 1869

18. Ulysses S. Grant – 1869 - 1877

   a.   Elihu B. Washburne – 1869

   b.   Hamilton Fish – 1869 – 1877

19. Rutherford B. Hayes - 1877 – 1881

   a. Hamilton Fish - 1877

   b, William M. Evarts - 1877 – 1881

20. James A. Garfield – 1881

   a. James G. Blaine 1881

21. Chester A. Arthur – 1881 – 1885

   a. James G. Blaine– 1881

   b. Frederick Theodore Frelinghuysen - 1881 – 1885

22. Grover Cleveland — 1885 – 1889

   a.   Thomas F. Bayard — 1885 – 1889

23. **Benjamin Harrison – 1889 – 1893**

    a. **William F. Wharton – 1892**

    b. **John W. Foster – 1892 - 1893**

    c. **William F. Wharton – 1893**

24. **Grover Cleveland – 1893 – 1897**

    a. **William F. Wharton - 1893**

    b. **Walter Q. Gresham – 1893-1895**

    c. **Edwin F. Uhl -1895**

    d. **Richard Olney 1895-1897**

25. **William McKinley – 1897 - 1901**

    a. **John Sherman - 1897 -1898**

    b. **William R. Day - 1898**

    c. **Alvey A. Adee - 1898**

    d. **John Hay – 1898 – 1901**

26. **Theodore Roosevelt – 1901-1909**

    a. **Francis B. Loomis 1901-1905**

    b. **Elihu Root – 1909-1909**

    c. **Philander C. Knox – 1909-1909**

27. **William Howard Taft - 1909-1913**

    a. **Philander C. Knox- 1909-1913**

28. **Woodrow Wilson – 1913-1921**

    a. **William Jennings Bryan 1913-1915**

    b. **Robert Lansing - 1915-1920**

    c. **Frank Polk – 1920**

    d. **Bainbridge Colby – 1920-1921**

29. **Warren G. Harding – 1921-1923**

    a. **Charles Evans Hughes – 1921-1923**

30. **Calvin Coolidge – 1929-1933**

    a. **Charles Evans Hughes - 1925-1929**

    b. **Frank B. Kellogg – 1929**

31 **Herbert Hoover – 1929-1933**

    a. **Frank B. Kellogg – 1929**

    b. **Henry L. Stimson – 1929-1933**

32. **Franklin D. Roosevelt – 1933-1945**

    a. **Cordell Hull – 1933-1944**

    b. **Edward Stettinius Jr. – 1944-1945**

33. **Harry S. Truman – 1945 – 1953**

    a. **James F. Byrnes – 1948-1947**

    b. **George C. Marshall – 1947-1949**

    c. **Dean Acheson – 1949-1953**

34. **Dwight D. Eisenhower – 1953 - 1961**

    a. **Harrison F. Matthews – 1953**

    b. **John Foster Dulles – 1953 – 1959**

    c. **Christian Herter - 1959-1961**

35. **John F. Kennedy – 1961-1963**

    a. **Livingston T. Merchant – 1961**

    b. **Dean Rusk – 1961-1963**

36 **Lyndon B. Johnson – 1963-1969**

    a. **Dean Rusk – 1963-1969**

37. **Richard Nixon – 1969-1973**

    a. **Charles E. Bohlen - 1969**

    b. **William P. Rogers - 1969 -1973**

    c. **Kenneth Rush – 1973**

    d. **Henry Kissinger – 1973-1977**

38. **Gerald Ford – 1974-1977**

   a. **Henry Kissinger 1974-1977**

39. **Jimmy Carter – 1977-1981**

   a. **Philip Habib – 1977**

   b. **Cyrus Vance – 1977-1980**

   c. **Warren Christopher – 1980**

   d. **David D. Newsomi – 1980**

   e. **Warren Christopher - 1980**

   f. **Edmund Muskie – 1980-1981**

40. **Ronald Reagan – 1981-1989**

   a. **Alexander Haig 1981-1982**

   b. **Walter J. Stoessel Jr – 1982**

   c. **George P. Shultz – 1982-1989**

41. **George H. W. Bush – 1989-1993**

   a. **Michael Armacost – 1989**

   b. **James Baker 1989-1992**

   c. **Lawrence Eagleburger – 1992-1993**

42. **Bill Clinton – 1993-2001**

   a. **Arnold Kanter – 1993**

Introduction

Well, here we are, another volume of, "The Writings of Antonio." The idea to write this book came to me in light of the current situation with Iran. Just days ago, President Trump ordered military strike upon Iranian general Soleimani, as he was taken out, along with another key official, by our air to ground missile strike on their entourage headed for no good. I sit watching the overview of our intelligence gathering and reports from current video streams provided by national news sources, and strategy overview moving forward,-- given by Secretary of State, Mike Pompeo; and I thought to myself, "Man, this is pretty serious, and I need to start paying more attention."

I mean, I was a junior in college at UCSD, during 9/11 and the Bush Administration, and I don't recall what I was doing when Osama Bin Laden was killed during Obama's term in Office. Nevertheless, today at 39, I think I need to do a better job of keeping up with the currents. Immediately, I acknowledged my own gap in knowledge in terms of US Presidential history as well as War Strategies implemented with and by their Secretaries of States for our country. I thought a little study was necessary and I might benefit from taking and producing some notes along the

way. Hence, Vol. III of the series, The Writings of Antonio, (US Presidents, Their Generals, and Their Wars.)

This study will not be comprehensive of all the
domestic, economic, and sociological issues going on
during each President's term, but will try to focus on
major foreign policy decisions with respect to the various Wars fought by our nation at home and abroad,
and if at all possible the strategies enacted by our
administration to be victorious. I hope I am not bit-
ing off more than I can chew, and understand that my
analysis or summation will be limited by my lack of
access to certain classified and military documents.

Chapter 1

George Washington

Well, here we are, the beginning of a journey through the study of the office of the American Presidency focusing on the wars and foreign policy matters under their leadership and administration. More specifically, the Presidents role as well as the role of their Secretary of State, weather minor or significant. Coincidentally, many of the Presidents had more than one Secretary of State serve during their term, so in an attempt to not be convoluted in my writing, I will try to be as concise as possible.

George Washington was born on February 22, 1732, and this is the day, or the third Monday of the month rather that we honor Washington's and Lincoln's birthday's for President's day, which was first officially recognized and celebrated in 1968. A little off topic for this book, but in light of the fact that I will not be talking much or focusing on the Atlantic Slave Trade or domestic issues during these periods of history, I would also like to highlight Carter G. Woodson, an African American educator, writer and Harvard Graduate, who pushed to implement a Black History Week, also in the month of February. Because of his initial efforts, all of the US Presidents since 1970, have recognized February as "Black History Month."

Under Washington's administration, aside from the Seven Year's War, which was a global war, so to speak, that expanded 5 continents and included multiple European Nations, Africa, India and the Philippines, there were pretty much one other war that we fought. Two major wars, many battles and squirmiest, that I will not go into, but they were obviously, the French and Indian War (1754–1763) and the American Revolution War (1775–1783).

The French and Indian war is considered essentially the American sphere of the Seven Year's War as America consisted of colonies of Britain and France, as well as allied Indians, or Native Americans.

The American Revolution was the historic battle of the 13 colonies against King George and the Great Britain Monarchy. Those in the states felt a bit taken advantage of because of the taxes levied by the crown, and ironically coined the phrase, "no taxation without representation." Sounds like a modern day rap lyric. As we fought for our Independence in battle with Great Britain, France came to our aide with money, resources, and Army and Navy reinforcements. French Naval ships were a major contribution to the sea front theater, as they blocked British navy from arriving and taking American ports.

There were four Secretaries of State that served during Washington's term. The first being John Jay, who was born on December 23, 1775 and was maternally home schooled until sent to an Anglican Priest for 3 years and then eventually went off to what is now Columbia University in his early teenage years. He ultimately studied law, started his own practice and among other details, found himself in the seat of the Secretary of State. Secretary John Jay implemented and pioneered a number of operational considerations to strengthen the colonies as a fledgling nation, as well as initiated a currency and credit system that could be recognized by certain European banks.

The second person to fulfill the role of the Secretary of State position under the Washington's administration was Thomas Jefferson, who also served as the third president. Jefferson served as an ambassador to France where he attempted to assist the French and negotiate with Britain on their behalf and interests. Also, there was dispute between Hamilton and Jefferson. Jefferson sought to expand a democratic –republic and was contrary to major banks having so much power in the colonies. Jefferson's education was very broad and he had a depth of many subjects. He started out by reading books from his father's library, and ultimately studied, history, philosophy, the classics, metaphysics, multiple science disciplines, agriculture, law, and even architecture.

Edmund Randolph was the third Secretary of State that served under Washington. Before his career on the president's staff he served as the Attorney General in the state Virginia. Randolph filled the Secretary of State position after the resignation of Jefferson and worked heavily on the Treaty of Amity or the Jay treaty in whitch trade, commerce and., nego tiation between the US and Britain was encouraged. Randolph was known to be a man of peace in terms of the tension between Jefferson and Hamilton.

Timothy Pickering was born on July 17, 1745 and was a Harvard Graduate. His politics can be described as opposite that of Jefferson, as he aligned with the Hamilton sentiment on the Federalist papers and in his own right was willing to go to War with France.

Chapter 2

John Adams

The second president of the soon to be independent nation was John Adams. Adams, helped bring the Revolutionary War to a close and thus was the first president to administrate under a completely independent nation, without Great Britain on the its back. Adams was trained as a lawyer, politician, and diplomat. He as President also fought against France in the Quest War (1798-1800).

After winds from the American Revolution settled, Adams found himself in another battle because the French attacked and stole a US ship off the east coast. This led to the legislative branch developing a Navy Department and for other officers to strengthen Army. This happening is ironic to me, considering we sent ambassadors to the French;==namely Jefferson, and secondly, France came to our aide in war against the British helping to establish our independence.

Once again in office, Timothy Picking also severed as Secretary of State during Adam's tenure. This time around, he supported close ties with Britain and as the UK Britain allied with France during the Napoleon Wars (1803-18-15). One policy implemented un der Picking's leadership was the Embargo Act of 1807, which was an embargo against any and all foreign nations that had intent to do harm to Britain or France during the Napoleon Wars. What's interesting is how quickly our allies changed from President to President.

Charles Lee was the second secretary of state under Adams, but His term was less than a year as he served longer as the US Attorney General (1795-1801).

John Marshall was the third Secretary of State and was given the responsibility to bring the Quasi War to an end. He accomplished this mission and later went to serve as a Chief Justice on the Supreme Court.

Chapter 3

Thomas Jefferson

As we see, the founding fathers often served in multiple government roles throughout their legal and political careers. Jefferson served in four main capacities, that is a member of congress, Minster to France, Secretary of State, and herein, President. I know that upon introduction I said that I would not touch on domestic economic issues, yet I think it should be noted that upon taking office, Jefferson took on a national debt of upward 80 milllion dollars and brought it down to under 60 million through a number of budgetary cuts, maneuvers, and downsizing of certain government offices; one such department being the Navy at the time considered by Jefferson in some ways to be unnecessary at it's current size during times of peace.

Interestingly enough, under Jefferson's leadership, America would fight a war on the Seas because of Pirates in those days raiding our ships and taking hostages and bounty, causing conflict. This war would be called the Barbary War, which was against Tripili a major city of Libya, and Jefferson ordered Navy forces to overtake them upon the Mediterranean Sea.

Something else worth mentioning was that Jefferson saw a need to establish military colleges where our own countrymen could study, amongst other things, topics like engineering that we would not have to have to depend so heavily upon foreign intelligence and ability from individuals who may not be as loyal. The resulting University that precipitated from this idea or Military Peace Establishment Act, was The United States Military Academy or West Point.

The first Secretary of State to serve under Jefferson was Levi Lincoln Sr. He, like many statesmen was a Harvard Graduate and also attained a law degree. Levi Lincoln was known to be particular when Jefferson wanted to declare war during the Barbary War, and recommend he first get permission from Congress. He also served as the United States Attorney General.

The second acting Secretary of State under Jefferson was James Madison. He was known to have a philosophical bent and helped write the federalist papers. Until now, I have not mentioned the Louisiana purchase, Madison was said to be the Supervisor of this matter.

Chapter 4

James Madison

We have covered Secretary of State Madison, and now we take a bit deeper look at his background and the war his administration was entangled with. To pick up from that which was aforesaid, that he was known to be philosophical, upon Completion of his studies at Princeton, He continued his education into political theory and political philosophy. He learned mathematics, Latin, Greek, and theology as a youth and young adult.

In terms of warfare, Madisson had to endure attacks on US eastern shores from Britain and their constant strategic economic means of subversively affecting the colonies thorough industry and commerce. Madison had strategies of his own, one being to attempt to pit Britain against France, and then sent means of delegation officers to Russia to have them arbitrate peace between the two sovereign nations. When these attempts weren't enough, Madison ultimately motioned to Congress for a declaration of War in 1812. It is thought that this was a type of second "war of Independence," And from the outside looking in, it seems that it was fought because Britain was trying to be a bit of a bully at the time, not letting go, even after the Revolutionary War was fought and won.

The First acting Secretary of State under Madison's administration was Robert Smith. He ultimately graduated from Princeton and went on to practice law in the Northeastern part of the Country. He had two major appointments; well I guess three, during his journey to becoming. He served as Secretary to the Navy, and then served in the capacity of Attorney General from, and finally Secretary of State. He was also was an Army Veteran himself, in combat during the Revolutionary War, under President Washington.

The second Secretary of State serving under President Madison was James Monroe. He was born April 28.1758 and was said to attend school only part time throughout the year because of his families need for him at home on the farm. After graduation from college, he eventually served as Congressmen, Senator, Governor of Virginia, Ambassador to France, Secretary of State, and President.

In the capacity of Secretary of State, he opposed Britain and French attacks on the eastern shores as did Robert Smith. Further, he tried to enact a treaty of which Britain refused to keep compliance, hence the War of 1812. He encouraged Navy Ship attack strategies to go on the offensive and move away from homeland ports. Eventually the Treaty of Ghent was signed by US and Great Britain which ended the War of 1812, and essentially legislated that the two sovereign nations would keep to their own bor-

ders

www.ingramcontent.com/pod-product-compliance
Lightning Source LLC
Chambersburg PA
CBHW021227090426
42740CB00006B/413